The Solution

A Blueprint for Change and Happiness

William Matta, Ed.D.

Idyll Arbor, Inc.

39129 264th Ave SE, Enumclaw, WA 98022 (360) 825-7797

Idyll Arbor, Inc. Editor: Sandra Swenby
© 2015 Idyll Arbor, Inc.

ISBN 9781611580440 paper
ISBN 9781611580457 e-book

Dr. William J. Matta
64 Newbury Drive
Southampton, New Jersey 08088
(856) 396-0080
willmed609@aol.com

Library of Congress Cataloging-in-Publication Data
Matta, William J.
  The solution : a blueprint for change and happiness / William Matta, Ed.D.
     pages cm
  ISBN 978-1-61158-044-0 (pbk.) -- ISBN 978-1-61158-045-7 (ebook)
  1.   Thought and thinking. 2.   Mind and body. 3.   Motivation (Psychology) I. Title.
  BF441.M3298 2015
  158--dc23
                                                    2015004048

I dedicate this book to my family — my wife, Alexia, of forty-one years; my son Lee and his wife Lori, and our two grandchildren, Keyley, age ten years, and Keaton, age eight years; and my son Kyle and his wife Kelly, and our grandson, Brody, age three years.

Last, I should mention our cat Buddy who sat by my side while I was writing this book.

Contents

Preface

I have been a psychotherapist in private practice and a college psychology professor for over twenty-five years. In my practice, I have applied a variety of techniques to help my clients deal with problems including depression, stress, anxiety, marriage, child-rearing, and toxic relationships.

As a result of this experience, I have found that some clinical modalities are extremely effective while others yield minimal benefits. During counseling sessions I often supplement therapy with books. Unfortunately, all too often my clients comment that the books are too technical, boring, or not practical.

I decided to write *The Solution: A Blueprint for Change and Happiness* to outline laws and principles that have been scientifically and clinically proven to produce quick, long-lasting, positive results in a user-friendly, insightful format.

The goal of this book is to enlighten and inspire you to implement permanent change and take control of your life. As a result, you will learn how to *emotionally reset* yourself. Changing feeling bad to feeling good is something you will be able to do.

Everyone wants to embrace happiness and their dreams — and can, if they only know how! For most people, achieving a state of well-being involves change. We stop ourselves from realizing our dreams, but that doesn't have to be the case. Often, we don't know how to change, or tend to resist change and become stuck in a state of depression, stress, or anxiety. Other times we do not know what steps to take to enhance our marriage, take charge of our children, or deal with a toxic relationship.

This book will tell you how. It is strategically divided into two sections.

Section I: The Solution (Chapters 1 through 7) introduces you to four pivotal laws and mind-changing techniques that have proven to be effective — and definitely more effective than medication — for achieving change and happiness. You will be introduced to proven laws, techniques, and simple exercises that will enlighten and empower you to change and take control of your life and destiny. You will learn how not to be a prisoner of your old dysfunctional thoughts.

Section II: A Blueprint for Change and Happiness (Chapters 8 through 12) shows you how to apply the information you learned in Section I to specific problems in your life, so you can take charge of your life and achieve your goals: confronting or terminating toxic relationships, taking charge of your children, improving your marriage, and reprogramming yourself for success.

I invite you to join me on this journey to learn how to implement change and gain the skills you need to achieve a peaceful, rewarding, and meaningful life. This book is called *The Solution* for a reason. It shows you the way to empower yourself so your visualizations really do come true.

— William Matta

Acknowledgments

I would like to thank Captain Dan Hoffman, LCSW, for writing Chapter 12 Taking Charge of an Abusive Relationship.

Special thanks to Mrs. Debra Stevenson for her patience, her ability to make sense of my handwriting, and the numerous hours she spent transcribing the manuscript.

Thanks to Mrs. Liz Fetzko for reviewing and modifying the manuscript.

Last, I am grateful to my wife, Alexia, for being so patient and understanding while I utilized countless hours of my free time to write the book.

Section I.
The Solution

1. Understanding the Nature of Change

When you suffer an attack of nerves, you're being
attacked by the nervous system. What chance has a
person against a system?
                                   — *Russell Hoban, American author*

I am a psychotherapist. I have been in private practice for over 25 years and have treated numerous clients for stress, anxiety, and depression. If those feelings are some of the reasons you picked up this book, I can help you, too.

The majority of my clients who suffered from anxiety and panic attacks believed that their so-called nervous breakdown was attributable to "weak nerves," and that they had no control over this powerful, devastating force. They often felt like they were going crazy.

If you have similar feelings, you will be relieved to learn that nerves do not break down and that you are not going crazy.

Crazy is not a psychological term, but it is often confused with the term *psychosis*. Two of the major criteria for psychosis are hallucinations and delusions. Hallucinations are false sensory impressions, such as seeing or hearing things that don't exist. Delusions are false beliefs; for example, you think you are Moses. If you're not having these symptoms, you're in the right place.

Beyond my professional work, I understand at a personal level what may be happening to you. About 30 years ago, I personally suffered from anxiety and panic attacks. At that time I was a sales manager for a Fortune 500 company. My wife and I had two young children. She was a homemaker and was going to nursing school part-time. During that time,

I wanted to continue my education and pursue a career as a psychotherapist, but for financial reasons it wasn't feasible. All of a sudden, out of nowhere, I feared crossing bridges.

Whenever I approached or was crossing a bridge, I would get dizzy and feel faint, and experienced rapid breathing, heart palpitations, and chest pains. This was so intense that I would speed over the bridge to escape the situation. If I knew then what I know today about anxiety and panic attacks, I would have known what to do to relieve them.

Maybe you don't go into full panic-attack mode. Even so, your worries, your fears, your anxiety, and your underlying stress all keep you from living the best life you can. There are changes you can make so you can achieve your dreams. It all starts with knowing how to deal with your attitudes about stress.

> Mental tensions, frustrations, insecurity, aimlessness are among the most damaging stressors, and psychosomatic studies show how often they cause migraine headaches, peptic ulcers, heart attacks, hypertension, mental disease, suicide, or just hopeless unhappiness.
>
> — *Hans Seyle*

In case you are wondering, dealing with stress effectively is very important. Hans Seyle's discovery of the physiological mechanism of stress led to today's understanding of how stress is a major contributor to coronary artery disease, cancer, respiratory disorders, cirrhosis of the liver, proneness to accidents, and suicide. Stress can aggravate other mental and physical conditions such as diabetes, multiple sclerosis, herpes, high blood pressure, drug abuse, family discord, and violence, as well as mental illness.

Stress is actually a result of any circumstance that threatens, or is perceived to threaten, our well-being and coping ability.

In this definition of stress, the operative word is *threaten*. Today, mental health professionals understand it's not so much what happens to us that causes stress; it's our interpretation of what is happening to us that really matters. The stress cycle operates as follows. We perceive a situation as threatening, we become fearful or angry, and our emergency physical response system is activated.

It's not stress that is killing us; it's our reaction to it.

— *Hans Seyle*

One of my clients, Steven, became terrified whenever he was forced to shop at the mall. When he entered the mall, he thought he would faint, have a heart attack, and lose total control of himself. For the majority of us, going to a mall is not a terrifying experience, unless we charge too much on our account. For Steven, however, a trip to the mall was (perceived as) a threat to his well-being, causing fear which activated his emergency response system. This stressful act produced anxiety and panic. As always happens with panic, Steven developed a case of the *what ifs* about going to the shopping center, "What if I get dizzy and faint?" "What if I have a heart attack?" "What if I lose control and go crazy and people see it?" "What if...?"

Most people don't realize it's not the specific feared situation that causes the panic reaction. It's our thoughts that actually cause it. More specifically, it's the *what ifs* that trigger the flight response, the response to escape from the mall. In essence, as you'll learn in this book, once you terminate the *what ifs,* there will be no more anxiety and panic. It was not the stress of the experience that caused Steven's anxiety and panic. It was his perception of the situation that caused it.

Even in the 1930s, Seyle understood that it is our mind, or, more specifically, our own thoughts that are killing us. It's our thoughts that activate our emergency response system. Our nervous system cannot tell the difference between true threatening situations and imagined ones. Our nervous system cannot tell the difference between what is true and not true; therefore what we perceive as being true is truth to our emergency response system, which regulates all involuntary muscles and glands. This part of the nervous system prepares us for fight or flight, and can even cause panic attacks.

> The components of anxiety, stress, fear, and anger do not exist independently of you in the world. They simply do not exist in the physical world, even though we talk about them as if they do.
> — *Wayne Dyer, psychotherapist and author*

The great majority of stress is created within ourselves. I emphasize to my clients, especially to the ones that suffer from extreme stress, anxiety, and panic, that the emergency fight-or-flight response system cannot distinguish between actual threats and perceived threats. If we perceive a situation as threatening, no matter how minor it is, it functions as a real threat, and the emergency response system is activated. We can hyperventilate, experience chest pains, have heart palpitations, and feel faint and terrified. We can also have choking sensations, bronchial spasms, and feel unable to cope.

You will be pleased to learn that *if your mind can cause these terrifying sensations, your mind can also take them away.* Many therapists feel that, except for situations which could cause actual physical harm to a person, no place, thing, or person should be able to *cause* you to behave in a certain way. It's our interpretation of the situation that causes our reaction. It's how we perceive the world that causes unnecessary stress and anxiety. The components of fear and anxiety do not exist independently in our world. They simply do not exist in the physical world.

It comes down to how we look at things. For example, you are about to interview for a job you really need or want. You can look at the upcoming interview as intimidating or threatening, which in turn causes fear, stress, and anxiety; or you can view it as a golden opportunity.

During these difficult economic times, numerous people are forced into a position where they have to make career changes. Incidentally, statistics show that the average person makes seven complete career changes in a lifetime. You can perceive a career change as fearful or threatening, or you can view it as a new, refreshing opportunity to reinvent yourself, even though it may involve enrolling in courses or additional training to reach your goals.

Initially many of my clients say that the concepts I will present to you here are not realistic or obtainable. As I work with these clients, they come to see how realistic the concepts are. I guarantee you that if you follow the guidelines in this book, you will not only understand why they work to change your life, you will actually adopt them as a way of living, a style of life.

> The longer I live, the more I realize the impact of
> attitude on life. Attitude is more than facts. It is more
> important than the past, than education, than money,
> than circumstances, than failures, than successes, than
> what other people think or say or do. It is more
> important than appearances, giftedness, or skill. It will
> make or break a company — a church — a home. The

> remarkable thing is we have a choice everyday regarding
> the attitude we will embrace for that day. We cannot
> change our past — we cannot change the fact that
> people will act in a certain way.
>
> — *Charles Swindoll, educator and author*

Our attitudes affect us and also can affect our families. An example of how attitudes can break a family is that of Robert and Rachael. Robert entered the office in a confused and frantic state. He proclaimed that his wife, Rachael, informed him that she wanted a divorce over an incident that happened 15 years ago. They had been married for 16 years and they had one daughter, age 13.

About six months prior to our meeting, Robert felt guilty about an indiscretion that took place six months into their marriage. He was on a business trip in Atlantic City and he had dinner with a woman that he had met during a convention. There was nothing intimate nor were there any sexual advances. After years of agonizing about the situation, he decided to unburden his soul by telling his wife. A few weeks after his confession, he was shocked when his wife told him that she could not forgive him and that she had filed for divorce. Robert pleaded with her to participate in the counseling process in hope of resolving the issue, but as I hear too often, she felt that she didn't have the problem, he did.

Although I have never met Rachael, it was very likely that her decision to divorce was a result of unconscious family-of-origin issues revolving around abandonment and loyalty, most likely stemming from her father's abandonment of her mother when Rachael was young. What was most disconcerting and frustrating was the fact that, with the exception of one indiscretion, both felt they had a good marriage. Today both are single and the only time they communicate is to discuss matters about their child.

Granted, Robert should never have had a "secret" dinner with another woman, but his wife's decision to terminate the marriage was a result of an irrational, even dysfunctional, belief, an attitude that destroyed the family.

Many people feel that they are too stressed out to even consider adopting a positive attitude and that it cannot be changed. That feeling simply isn't true. Self-defeating attitudes can change, and you have a daily choice of the attitude you embrace to take charge of your life.

You cannot control your past or change your past. You can only change your reaction to past events by changing your attitude. I am convinced that life is 10% what happens to us and 90% how we react to it. Stress, anxiety, and fear do not have to control your life.

You have chosen to read this book because you want to change your life. You want to eliminate needless stress and worry. You want to alleviate depression and anxiety, or maybe you want to discover better ways to deal with relationships, your marriage, and your future. If you follow the simple rules and principles outlined in this book, you will achieve your goals. Let's look at the first step to overcome stress, anxiety, and depression, and acquire the ability to master your emotional state.

Adopting the Right Attitude

It is our attitude at the beginning of a difficult undertaking, which more than anything else will determine its successful outcome.

— *William James, philosopher and psychologist*

Any new adventure will cause us some anxiety. Anxiety is fear of the unknown; it is impossible to know exactly what the future holds. My experience is that our attitude is the primary factor in determining our future. Attitude determines whether we succeed or fail.

A human being is not one thing among others; things determine each other but man is ultimately self-determining. What he becomes — within the limits of endowment and environment — he has made out of himself. In the concentration camps, for example, in this living laboratory and on this testing ground, we watched

and witnessed some of our comrades behave like swine
while others behaved like saints. Man has both
potentials within himself; which one is actualized
depends on decisions but not on conditions.

> *— Victor Frankl, psychiatrist, author,*
> *and concentration camp survivor*

You create your life through your thoughts. It's your thoughts and attitudes, not external events, which create your existence. Even though Dr. Frankl was subjected to atrocities while held a prisoner in a concentration camp, with determination and the right attitude he was able to not only survive the ordeal but also to transcend his environment.

Fear, stress, and anxiety are individual responses or potential reactions to any given situation. They do not exist in the physical world. Again, it's not so much what happens to us that matters, it's our perception or interpretation of the situation that matters. It is a fact that most people would rather die than give a speech in front of a large crowd. If you perceive such an act as threatening and potentially embarrassing, you will probably stumble through the speech. On the other hand, if you are well prepared and focus your thoughts on the act being a great opportunity to get your point across, the speech will be a success. All of us have within us the ability to maximize our potentials; half the battle is making the decision to do so.

You cannot change or resolve your problems by using the same kind of thinking you used to create them. My experience as a therapist has shown me that the major reason people become overwhelmed by feelings of hopelessness, despair, and helplessness is because their way of thinking becomes stuck. Mental health therapists understand that your thoughts determine how you feel and behave. Depressed, fearful, and anxious people think in depressed, fearful, and anxious ways. Your thoughts, not your circumstances, determine how you live and conduct your life. Let's look at one of the thought processes that doesn't work.

Worry

Worry means to torment yourself with disturbing thoughts. Worry is tense, unproductive thinking about things over and over again. It's the disturbing thoughts that torment us. We need to learn a healthier, more realistic way to think because most of the things we worry about never happen. Worry is tension; worry is repetitive thinking. Worry is self-inflicted tension that is self-defeating, and that does not produce desired results. Worry is a cycle of inefficient thought revolving around a pivot of fear.

I often ask my clients to try to recall worries they had a year ago. Most can't remember any unless there was a major tragic event, such as illness or death of a loved one. The majority of the things we thought were so critical cannot be remembered months later. What a waste of precious time — people gather bundles of sticks to build bridges that they never cross.

As we'll see in Chapter 8 Taking Charge of Your Anxiety, needless worry is a major factor in producing anxiety. The underlying theme in anxiety is magnification — the *what ifs*. People with anxiety who also suffer from panic attacks typically focus their thoughts on the worst possible outcome. They typically utilize the *what ifs*: "What if I stutter during my presentation?" "What if I have an attack in the mall?" "What if I get fired?" "What if I make a fool of myself?" Anxiety also causes us to lose perspective and then perceive instructions as threatening or dangerous. This faulty thinking leads to a lack of ability to distinguish the difference between threatening and non-threatening situations.

> If I had to live my life over I would have more actual troubles, but I'd have fewer imaginary ones.
>
> — *Don Herald, author*

How often do we see problems as rocks or boulders when in reality they turn out to be pebbles? How often does useless stress and worry cause conflict not only with us, but also with our families, loved ones, and children?

A successful technique that I utilize in my practice to help alleviate needless worry is to help people distinguish between the terms *possible* and *probable*. For example, a young teen female was constantly consumed with thoughts about her parents dying in a car accident. These thoughts existed because her cousin died tragically in a car accident a few years before. These thoughts were so paralyzing that she had difficulty sleeping, studying, and socializing. During one of her sessions, we discussed the possible-versus-probable concept. I asked her if it was possible for a meteorite to strike this office. She replied yes. I then asked her if it is probable. Her response was no. Was it possible her parents could die in a car accident? She said yes. I repeated was it probable? Her answer was no. The odds that her parents could die today were ten thousand to one. Such a scenario has helped many of my clients eliminate needless worry over unlikely events.

> There are only two ways to live your life. One is as though nothing is a miracle. The other is as though everything is a miracle.
>
> — *Albert Einstein*

One of the definitions of a miracle is any wonderful or amazing thing, fact, or event. Continue reading so you can bring about the miracle of transforming your life and enabling yourself to achieve things you never thought possible.

Keeping Track of Your Progress

As you go through the book, you will want to keep notes of important points — that's how you can remember them when you need to practice making a change. There will also be places where you will be asked to write down your current thoughts about something like what you want from life — that's how you know what you want to change. There are a few quizzes that measure things like your current level of stress. You will want to keep track of those scores — that's how you know that you have changed.

You may be able to make notes right in the text, but that makes it difficult to share the book with others. It is probably better to keep a paper or electronic journal that is separate from this book. You may be dealing with some issues you would rather keep private, and a separate journal is more effective at keeping others from reading your thoughts.

Regardless of how you keep your notes, it is very important that you actually do keep them. It's hard for people to remember how they felt in the past. Somewhere along the line you might be discouraged at your rate of change. With notes, you will have a reminder of where you started from and will be able to see how much progress you really have made, even if you still have a ways to go.

> Let's start with a really simple note. Write down a number between 0 and 10 that represents how big a part worry and anxiety play in your daily life. Zero means that worry and anxiety are not part of your life. Ten means that you're in constant panic mode — your whole life and all your energy are consumed by your worries and anxieties.

Solution Summary

- Change can be perceived as a new, refreshing opportunity to reinvent yourself.
- The stress cycle: When you perceive an event as threatening, you become fearful, and your emergency fight-or-flight system is activated.
- The only place to break the stress cycle is in your thoughts.
- It's your thoughts, how you look at and think about things, that activate your emergency response system.
- Stress, anxiety, and fear do not have to control your life.
- The great majority of stress is created within yourself.
- Worry is tension and unproductive thinking about things in repetitive ways.
- Make notes to keep track of your progress. You won't realize how far you have come if you don't keep track of where you started.

2. Conquering the Fear of Change

Intelligence is the ability to adapt to old and especially new situations.

— *Author unknown*

There are many definitions of intelligence. The definition that makes the most sense to me and that I teach to my clients is that intelligence is the ability to adapt to old and, especially, to new situations.

We all know people who have a high IQ, people who are extremely book smart, but have great difficulty coping in the real world. They may be geniuses who can easily do complex calculations, but they have difficulty dealing with people and solving their own numerous interpersonal or personal problems.

In my opinion, people who can adapt to their environment are the ones who are intelligent. They have the ability to deal with and even possibly transcend their environment. Intelligent people are able to change and adapt their lives as necessary. Inept people become traumatized by their fear of the unknown and are not able to take charge of the direction of their lives. Inept people get bounced around because they are not able to regulate their emotions.

A popular though unscientific definition of insanity is doing the same thing over and over again, while expecting different results. Theresa was an attractive, 34-year-old business executive who turned down a number of promotions because each required her to relocate out of state. Theresa still lived with her parents. She wouldn't move out of the house for fear of what her alcoholic father might do to her mother.

When her father drank too much, he became obnoxious and verbally abusive to her mother. Theresa learned at an early age to be the peacemaker of the family. She would often protect her mother by physically coming between her parents when an argument erupted. Sometimes her intervention worked, but usually it only served to escalate her father's fury.

When Theresa would threaten to leave, her mother would plead with her to stay. Out of guilt, Theresa felt obligated to remain at home. The dysfunctional family scenario lasted for years until her father, in an alcoholic rage, physically abused both Theresa and her mother. The police arrived; her father was arrested and slapped with a restraining order. Her father was not allowed to return home, and he was forced to get help for his drinking problem.

During his sobriety, he finally realized the negative impact his drinking inflicted on his family. As of today, he has not had a drink for three years. At last, Theresa felt secure enough to move out on her own. Undoubtedly, if it weren't for the police intervention and court action, this family would still be acting out their old self-defeating behavioral patterns.

Through counseling, Theresa realized that she was not responsible for her mother's happiness and that what we try to control often backfires. Theresa also learned, as do most adult children of alcoholics, that she had developed a codependent personality, including the trait of valuing others' opinions about how she should conduct her life more than her own beliefs. She compromised her own values and integrity to avoid rejection and the disapproval of others. She did not perceive herself as a lovable, worthwhile person. Using the guidelines outlined in this book, she learned to adapt to her situation. She learned how to change, find inner peace, and stop being the peacemaker. Most importantly, she learned to accept herself as a lovable, worthwhile person, and not to submit to others' demands.

Elizabeth provides another example of why it's critical to adapt to new situations. She initiated counseling because she was depressed. For many years she was a successful photographer, but due to modern technology, her income dropped from $90,000 to $20,000 a year. Her potential customers found it less expensive and easier to take and enhance their own digital pictures at weddings and other social events than to hire more expensive, professional photographers like her.

In spite of the reality of the situation, she frugally attempted to stay the course and stick with business as usual. In counseling, her despair gradually changed to the realization that she needed to adapt to a changing world. Fortunately her husband had a good job, and she was able to reinvent herself. Elizabeth entered nursing school at a local community college, and in a couple of years became a licensed RN.

Although she does not earn the income that she did at the peak of her photography career, she finds her work as a wound-care nurse emotionally secure and rewarding. It's interesting that community college enrollments are at their highest during difficult economic times. Apparently many people find it necessary and advantageous to reinvent themselves as a result of hard economic conditions. Elizabeth found the courage and openness to change her life and adapt to an ever-changing environment.

> Any change for the better is always accompanied by a
> certain amount of discomfort.
>
> — *Arnold Bennett*

People often resist change because they feel secure and somewhat comfortable with their fears, anxieties, depression, and unhappiness. It's not so much that they like this state, it's that they don't know how else to feel, and they don't realize that they have a choice. They don't know how to leave their dysfunctional comfort zone. Fear of making mistakes, fear of meeting new people, fear of going back to school, fear of looking stupid, fear of being happy — these are examples of thoughts that *create resistance* and further perpetuate feelings of hopelessness and despair.

It takes a certain amount of courage to release familiar discomfort and embrace something new and unfamiliar. There is no security in what is no longer meaningful. People who fear change actually are not secure within themselves and needlessly suffer. Change is inevitable, and those who initiate change are survivors who will have a better chance to manage the change that inevitably happens in our lives. Being adventurous and open to new experiences is more fulfilling that staying stuck. When you change for the better, you gain feelings of power and achievement — a feeling of security that you are living to your fullest potential.

In my field, we often encourage people to move away from their comfort zone. My clients discover that tension is a natural result of striving for growth and happiness. They eventually realize that, without a certain amount of tension, there is no growth.

Even positive change is stressful. One of the most stressful events is taking a vacation. Before you take a vacation, there is a lot to do: save money, make reservations, pack, make arrangements for pets, etc. Then you may have the hassles of air travel and car rental... and worry about what you might have forgotten to do.

Even a positive change in a family, such as when an alcoholic husband stops drinking, can produce catastrophic results without the right attitude. Many times when the alcoholic stops drinking, the couple breaks up.

What happens in so many alcoholic families is that the disease is insidious and gradually infiltrates the family. All too often, the non-alcoholic partner assumes the majority of the responsibilities for the family. The partner takes the children to sporting events, pays the bills, makes excuses for the alcoholic's absences, and is basically in charge of the family.

Once the alcoholic stops drinking and becomes sober, the family's balance dramatically changes as the recovering individual becomes more aware of family matters and may want to become more responsible and take more control. The dysfunctional arrangement that was established for years is disrupted, which generates high levels of anxiety and the possibility of divorce. Making so-called positive changes in our lives can be devastating if they aren't accompanied with a healthy attitude. But divorce does not have to be the outcome, if the family gets proper guidance while the alcoholic is attaining sobriety.

> It takes a lot of courage to release the familiar and
> seemingly secure, to embrace the new. But there is no
> security in what is no longer meaningful. There is more

security in the adventurous and exciting, for in
movement there is life, and in change there is power.
— *Alan Cohen*

So what you need now is the courage to change and the ability to change with a healthy attitude. You want to change to feel good about yourself, and to learn how to better handle stress, conquer depression and anxiety. When you move into the unknown, it is natural to feel uncomfortable. As you enter new waters, it may feel impossible to navigate, the waters don't feel natural, and you feel too far over your head.

Right this moment you may be creating your own resistance to overcoming your anxiety. For some people even thinking about change brings on panic attacks so devastating that they feel they can't breathe and that they will suffocate. No wonder these people feel that things can never change, and resist change with all their ability. Your anxiety might be that high, too. You may be thinking thoughts such as "Dr. Matta doesn't understand how my problems are unique." "I've been this way for years." "I've read self-help books before, and I still have panic attacks." "I'm beyond help." I have had clients even more anxious than that, and we have found ways for them to successfully change.

As a follow-up to the note you took in the previous chapter on your normal level of anxiety, make a note now, on the same 0 to 10 scale, about how you feel about making a change. Zero means you're ready to start — no problem. Ten means you're in a total panic even thinking that making a change is possible.

Even if your score is high, please read on. You'll find that it will get easier as you learn more about the process.

The life we want is not merely the one we have chosen
and made. It is the one we must be choosing and
making.
— *Wendell Berry*

My starting point is to help you realize what you can and cannot do. There is nothing you can do to change the past, so you must look at the present to make sure that the past does not repeat itself. One of the cognitive distortions or examples of faulty thinking that we will discuss in Chapter 6 is the *should haves*. For most people, the *should haves* cause overwhelming guilt.

> Take a moment and write a note listing your major *should haves*. Add a quick note on how they make you feel.

Our thoughts determine how we feel and, when we focus our thoughts on the *should haves*, we are bound to feel shame and sadness. The *should haves* are all about what's wrong with us: "I should have told her I loved her more." "I should have studied harder." "I should have behaved differently." "I should have taken that job." Instead of being open to change and instilling hope for the future, the *should haves* anchor us to our past and induce feelings of despair and hopelessness.

Emily's tragic story demonstrates how the *should haves* can actually kill us. Emily was an intelligent young girl who had big dreams for the future. She was a sophomore in high school when she fell in love with Tommy and became pregnant. Emily came from a religious family and, in a desperate effort to keep her pregnancy secret and keep peace with Tommy, she had an abortion. Emily was so tortured and guilt-ridden by her decision that she eventually turned to alcohol and drugs in a futile attempt to wipe out her shame. Life quickly spiraled down, and one night just before Christmas, she committed suicide (the third major cause of death in adolescents after unintentional accidents and homicide).[1] This senseless, tragic scenario probably could have been avoided if only Emily had gone to her parents or a mental health professional for help. Emily could have learned that although there was nothing that she could have done to change the past, she could have worked on the present to make positive changes in her life.

The Self-Defeating Cycle of Depression

Our thoughts determine how we feel, our feelings affect our behavior, and in turn the result of our behavior may create further feelings of depression and despair. Without help, many people continue to spiral more deeply into helpless and hopeless feelings.

Keaton's Struggle with Depression

When I first met him, Keaton was a severely depressed adolescent. He had been taking antidepressants for three years and his physician was about to prescribe an additional antidepressant. Keaton initially seemed skeptical that psychotherapy would do him any good or could alleviate his deep state of depression.

During our sessions, I learned that he was very religious to the point of being scrupulous. In uncovering the thoughts causing his resistance to recovery, I was surprised to learn that, even with medication, he constantly contrasted his behaviors and life to that of his higher supreme being.

I have counseled thousands of teens and Keaton was a fine, upstanding individual and an excellent student, but there was no way he could live up to his expectations of being like his higher supreme being. He found himself caught in the self-defeating cycle of depression: throughout his day he would focus on every flaw, such as envying another student or his dislike of another student, which only fueled his feeling of guilt, which caused him to spiral deeper and deeper into depression. At one point Keaton spiraled down to such deep depression that he attempted suicide because like thoughts attract like thoughts — negative thoughts attract more negative thoughts.

I was able to utilize the four laws that are outlined in the book to chip away at the negative thoughts that caused his resistance to recovery. Within a short period of time, he felt so good that he no longer needed any medication.

The Law of Association

One of the reasons that caused Keaton to spiral down to suicidal ideation was the Law of Association. The Law of Association says that like thoughts attract more like thoughts; thus, negative thoughts attract more negative thoughts. For example, think about something or someone that makes you unhappy. The more you think about it, the worse the scenario becomes. That's because negative thoughts act like a magnet to attract more negative thoughts. Conversely, positive thoughts attract more positive thoughts.

Keaton compared himself to his higher supreme being and his self-talk included thoughts like "I'm no good." "I shouldn't have envied that girl." "I sinned when I got angry at Carl." "Why can't I be a better person?" "I'm doomed to Hell."

As you will learn in Chapter 4, Keaton learned a sure way to identify when he was using the Law of Association to perpetuate negative thinking — and how to stop this! Most people don't want to be depressed or anxious. Most people don't want to worry needlessly. Most people don't want to feel that their future is hopeless. The Law of Association is the first of the four laws that can change your life forever. As you read on, you will find how you can change the thoughts that are creating your resistance to taking charge of your emotional and personal life.

> When we inwardly change our attitude, we not only see
> life differently, but life itself will come to be different.
> — *Katherine Mansfield*

Your life is in your hands. You can change your life by consciously choosing your thoughts. When you focus on and celebrate good feelings, you'll attract more good thoughts and good things in your life. When you start to feel good, you tend to make it a habit and you will see life differently. You will then approach life in a positive way — and naturally your life will change for the better. You will learn that happiness is a choice.

There will be more details later on how to do this, but here's an example of how making a change also changes the way we view things and makes the things we view change. I taught a psychology course from 2:00 to 5:00 PM on a Friday. Frankly, by Friday I'm exhausted and I would rather be anywhere but at work — and the students feel the same way. I knew that if I projected exhaustion onto the class, they would pick up on it and would become bored, restless, and inattentive. In turn, I would pick up on their negativity, which would make me feel more negative and invalidated — and so forth and so on. I realized that if I purposely and consciously projected energy and enthusiasm, the class would become energized, enthusiastic, and more eager to learn. This technique worked on the vast majority of the class — some students will never get enthusiastic about learning under any circumstances.

A similar scenario is true for couples. If you want your spouse to change, you must change. If you want your spouse to be more considerate, you must be considerate.

If we want the world to change, we must change. When you change, the way you view things changes, and the things you view change.

> When you change, the way you view things changes, and the things you view change.

There is no security or comfort in the world if your life does not seem meaningful or purposeful to you. You must decide what you want. Don't concentrate on what you fear or don't want. Think in a positive way about what you want from life.

> Take a few minutes to write a list of what you want from life in your personal journal. Consider various aspects of your life including relationships, marriage, career, children, etc.

As you read this book, keep this list nearby and modify it as necessary. You will come to realize that when you stay focused on what you want, you will create your future and your life. In reading this book, you will create a blueprint to completely change every aspect of your life by changing the way you think and approach life. Making a list is like creating an instruction manual for positive change.

SOLUTION SUMMARY

- Conquering the fear of change is the first step.
- Intelligence is the ability to adapt to old and, especially, new situations.
- It's your thoughts — your ways of thinking — that create your resistance to change.
- There is nothing you can do to change the past, so you have to look at the present to make sure the past does not repeat itself.
- The Law of Association: Like thoughts attract like thoughts.
- When you change, it changes the way you view things, and the things you view change.
- Listing the positive things you want is writing a roadmap for your change.

3. Our Thoughts Affect Our Bodies, Our Bodies Affect Our Lives

Our emotional life is physical; it makes imprints on our limbic system. When we have problems in our deep limbic system of the brain, it's manifested in moodiness, irritability, clinical depression, decreased motivation, and sleep problems.

— Dr. David Amen

The limbic system at the center of the brain is our emotional processing center. It consists of a complex of primitive evolutionary structures located on top of the brain stem and under the cortex. These limbic structures are involved with our emotions, motivations, and long-term memory, particularly related to survival. They control behaviors related to fear, anxiety, despair, anger, eating, and sexuality. Repeated negative self-talk and undue stress play havoc on our limbic system and can induce anxiety, irritability, clinical depression, social isolation, lack of motivation, and sleep problems.[2]

When my clients initially start counseling for depression and anxiety, they often complain that they are irritable, moody, anxious, lack motivation, have sleep problems, and experience increased or decreased appetite. They may be skeptical about what I have to offer and feel they can't be helped. They may feel that they have no control over their emotional states, and that they are doomed to an existence laden with despair, depression, and anxiety. Too often I hear "It is what it is!" and "My life and my future are hopeless and bleak." If you think about that thought "it is what it is," no wonder they are drowning in feelings of hopelessness and despair. Our thoughts determine how we feel. Continuing this kind of thinking destines us to an unfulfilled, uneventful, hopeless existence.

> Thoughts make chemicals. If you have happy thoughts
> you are producing chemicals that make you feel happy.
> If you have negative, depressing, pessimistic, or insecure
> thoughts, you are producing chemicals that make you
> feel depressed.
>
> — *Dr. Joseph Despenza, neuroscientist*

Your thoughts make brain chemicals that impact your life and actually change your body chemistry.

> *Our thoughts determine how we feel.*

When you feel threatened, your brain releases norepinephrine and you become tense, anxious, and your pulse rate increases. Every time you have a good thought, a hopeful, happy thought, or a thought of gratitude, your brain releases chemicals that literally make you feel good and calm you down via your limbic system. Your muscles relax, your heart beats more slowly, you breathe more slowly, and you become calm.[3]

You actually feel what you think! When you habitually think negative or self-defeating thoughts, your serotonin levels may decrease, producing depression and/or anxiety, and the levels of other brain chemicals may also go out of balance. These brain chemicals are called neurotransmitters, which carry information from one brain cell to another and are involved in the regulation of moods, eating, and sleeping.

We know that people who suffer from depression and anxiety may have insufficient levels of serotonin in their brain and/or imbalances in other neurotransmitters. Some antidepressant medications — such as the selective serotonin reuptake inhibitors (SSRIs), including Prozac (fluoxetine), Paxil (paroxetine), and Zoloft (sertraline) — reduce depression and anxiety by increasing the brain's serotonin level. Norepinephrine, serotonin, and some other neurotransmitters have been implicated not only in depression, but also in other types of mood and anxiety disorders.[4]

According to Dr. Caroline Leaf, 85% to 95% of the physical and mental illnesses we experience are a direct result of our thoughts. Negative thoughts create conditions for illness. For example, fear alone

> *85% to 95% of the physical and mental illnesses we experience are a direct result of our thoughts.*

triggers more than 1,400 chemical responses and 30 different hormones that can actually make us sick.[5]

> If you are someone who thinks sad, angry, or negative thoughts most of the day, you are weakening your immune system.
>
> — *Cathy Chapman, LCSW and author*

The immune system is a network of cells, tissues, and organs that work together to defend against tiny organisms that cause infections. The immune system is the body's surveillance and security system. It detects and eliminates disease-causing agents in the body, such as viruses and potentially damaging bacteria. If you are someone who thinks angry or negative thoughts most of the day, you are decreasing chemicals in your body that fight off infection.[6]

Stress and the Immune System

Today, scientists understand the relationship between the body's hormonal system and the onset and acceleration of both mental and physical diseases such as heart disease, infectious diseases, diabetes, asthma, gastric ulcers, headaches, depression, anxiety, and autoimmune diseases such as multiple sclerosis.

The immune system consists of billions of cells that travel through the bloodstream. They move in and out of tissues and organs, defending the body against foreign bodies (antigens) such as bacteria, viruses, and cancer cells. There are two types of cells called lymphocytes: B-cells and

T-cells. B-cells produce antibodies, which are released into the fluid surrounding the body's cells to destroy invading viruses and bacteria. T-cells are activated once the invader gets inside a cell. T-cells latch onto the infected cell, multiply, and destroy it.

Production of the hormone *cortisone* by the adrenal gland is increased by stress. Cortisone can suppress the effectiveness of the immune system by actually lowering the number of lymphocytes, thus the immune system's ability to fight off antigens is greatly reduced.

People who think positively produce a more normal amount of cortisone as well as feeling less stress.[7] It's a healthier way to live.

Stress Has Three Negative Effects

Stress has an effect on the digestive system. During stress, digestion is inhibited but the muscle activity of the bowels often increases. Adrenaline (epinephrine) released from the adrenal gland during stress may cause ulcers.

Stress increases heart rate and raises blood pressure. Consistently raised blood pressure over as little as several weeks is a major factor in coronary heart disease, causing heart failure and heart attacks.

Stress can also have a devastating direct and indirect influence on the immune system. People who use unhealthy coping mechanisms revert to overeating, drinking alcohol, and/or smoking tobacco to reduce stress.

> Happiness isn't just a vague ineffable feeling; it is a
> physical state that the brain can induce deliberately.
>
> — *Dr. Brian Knutson,*
> *professor of psychology and neuroscience*

Current research in the neurosciences provides clear evidence that by rehearsing the ways we change our thoughts from negative to positive, we can consistently rewire old negative circuits within the brain to become positive circuits. The more we activate specific brain areas via positive thinking, the more positive neural connections form in those areas, enabling the neurons (brain cells) involved to transmit their messages more efficiently.[8]

Negative emotions such as fear, despair, and anger help
us survive, while positive emotions such as curiosity, joy,
and gratitude let us thrive.

— Dr. Barbara Fedrick, neuroscientist

In addition to making you feel bad, depressed, and/or anxious, your
negative emotions place a burden on your physical and mental life.
However, there is a silver lining in negative feelings — if you evaluate
your negative experiences and formulate a contrast to your positive ones,
you can better appreciate and enjoy your positive emotions. The negative
emotions, which cause you to feel bad, can serve as a reference point for
change.

You cannot avoid negative feelings, they are a part of reality and
everyday living, but stressful negative events can provide you with an
opportunity to utilize the skills outlined in this book to become more
resilient at dealing with stressful situations and negative emotions. They
literally give you the opportunity to rewire your brain. I often tell my
clients that it isn't so much what happens to you that's important — it's
how you look at things! And remember that when you are more
optimistic and feel less stress, your body releases less potentially harmful
chemicals, and you are less likely to develop mental and physical
problems.

Coping With Stress

I cannot always control what goes on outside. But I can
always control what goes on inside.

— Dr. Wayne Dyer

In my practice I have seen firsthand the brutal results of stress on
people, both physically and mentally — depression, anxiety, high blood
pressure, ulcers, irritable bowel syndrome, etc. On the other hand,
without stress our lives would be unrewarding, empty, and boring.

In appropriate amounts, stress is stimulating and motivates us to accomplish things. Stress motivates us to make money. It motivates us to be a better student, marriage partner, parent, and friend. Stress motivates us to further our education or learn a trade and inspires us to better ourselves.

Your goal should not be a life without stress. The idea is to have the right amount of stress. You experience "good" stress when you feel you have some control over the stressful situation.[9]

The duration of the stressor and your perception of the stressor will determine its impact on you, the most critical factor being your perception of the situation. If you view the event to be threatening, the fight-or-flight survival mechanism in your brain will be activated and you will go into emergency survival mode. The more threatened you feel, the more helpless and less capable you will be to handle and cope with the problem. When you reach a certain point, you start catastrophizing, and begin to experience anxiety and even panic attacks. Your focus or attention narrows and restricts you to survival behaviors.

The critical factor for coping with stress is the ability to regulate the negative, survival-related emotions such as fear, sadness, despair, and anxiety. As you learn to regulate your negative emotions, you are literally blocking signals to parts of the limbic system in your brain, thereby quieting fear and anxiety. This action paves the way for you to calm down and figure out a way to better deal with the stressful situation.

Positive emotions enable you to broaden your focus, creatively problem-solve, and enhance your ability to be flexible in dealing with

> *You can actually learn to emotionally reset yourself.*

stress and trauma. This ability to regulate your emotions allows you to *act and not just react*. It permits you to make rational, sound decisions.[10] You can actually learn to *emotionally reset* yourself. Three techniques that work well are Reframing, Load Shedding, and Accepting. We'll look at those next.

Reframing

By altering your perception of the stressor, you can shift or reset your response to be more positive by changing or *reframing* your perception of the stressful situation from a threat to a challenge. By getting into a habit of changing your view of a stressful event from a threat to a challenge, you keep yourself from going into emergency mode. You learn to stress-proof your brain, and you raise your overall stress threshold.[11]

Reframing permits you to view a stressful event or events from a more positive context, which allows you to view the event(s) as more of a

> Ask yourself: Is there a better way to look at this problem?

challenge than an overwhelming threat. It enables you to deal with the situation in a better way.

> At this point in your journey for change and happiness, take some time and list a few of the stressors or traumas in your life in your journal. Then challenge your thoughts about those negative or stressful situations and replace them with more positive and realistic thoughts. Ask yourself: Is there a better way to look at this problem? Is there something I can learn from this experience? What is the silver lining? Is the situation in my control?

Here are some examples of reframing:

EXPERIENCE: "I lost my job. I'll never work again."
REFRAME: "It was a dead-end job anyway. I'll collect unemployment, go to community college for retraining, and find a better job."

EXPERIENCE: "My girlfriend said I never listen to her. Our relationship is over."
REFRAME: "This is my opportunity to show her I'm listening to her. I'll sincerely ask her what she wants from me that she is not getting."

EXPERIENCE: "My teenage daughter's behavior is out of control. I'll never be able to take charge."

REFRAME: "Her brain is still growing. She's only a teen. I'll find ways to take control."

EXPERIENCE: "No matter what I do, Kathy doesn't like me."
REFRAME: "I tried long enough to win her approval. It seems the situation is out of my control. I can't do anything about it."

In essence, by reframing the stressor you view stressful events more as a challenge that is doable or, in the last example about Kathy, as something to let go of.

Load Shedding

A technique that my clients find effective in reducing stress is what I call *load shedding*.

In the world of electrical power, load shedding can be used in commercial establishments such as supermarkets and office buildings to temporarily turn off equipment at

> *If you find your stress is approaching your peak level — load shed.*

times of peak demand on the power grid, thus saving on peak electrical use and preventing small and large power outages. Typical load shedding consists of temporarily turning off refrigeration compressors or dimming lights in the building.

The same concept can be applied to reducing stress. At certain times in your life, if you feel that your stressors are becoming insurmountable, load shed! If you find that your stress level is peaking, shed some stressors. For example, take a day off from work or spend extra time at a hobby.

If taking time off feels like it will just make things worse, there is another strategy to try. Drop a task. Find something you don't really need to do. Just like the *should haves* in your past, there are a lot of *should do's* in the present. There are things you must do — that's basic survival. However, there are probably things that only get to the level of *should do*. When your stress level is peaking, those are the things you should put off until later, or assign to someone else.

Once your stress level peaks, it becomes more difficult to emotionally reset yourself because you are stuck in survival mode. At this point you are living in a state of fear, anxiety, despair, depression, confusion, and irritability. All of your work suffers and you are much less efficient. So in the future, if you find your stress is approaching your peak level, load shed. It's a way to get more done, instead of less,

Accepting Stress and Pain

Instead of backing away or trying to escape from your negative emotions — fear, anger, despair, anxiety, etc. — first accept them.

Acknowledge how you are feeling without rushing to change the disturbing emotional state. Too often, people attempt to escape

> *Happy people acknowledge that life has its ups and downs*

uncomfortable feelings by rushing to alcohol, drugs, or tobacco, only to use addictive behavior to deal with stress. Happy, flourishing people don't run from their negative emotions. They acknowledge that life has its ups and downs and they confront life's pressures head on.

Mentally healthy people learn how to transform anger into motivation for positive behavioral changes.[12] They may reframe their anger at an insulting coworker as an opportunity to learn how to become more assertive and stick up for themselves. They may take a partner's disparaging remark, for example, about not spending enough time with the children, and reframe their feelings of guilt from threat to challenge, then seeing the challenge as an opportunity for positive change.

People who learn to tolerate unpleasant emotions for a few minutes, and who frequently use reframing as a cognitive reappraisal technique to alter their emotional reaction to stress and trauma, report greater psychological well-being than those who don't use such techniques.[13]

Resiliency

Resilience is the ability to modulate and constructively harness the stress response – a capacity essential to both physical and mental health.

— Dr. Steven Southwick and Dr. Dennis Charyney

Resiliency is the ability to bounce back when life hits you with lemons, and then make lemonade. Research has shown that the most effective way to combat stressors, such as medical problems, difficulties on your job, relationships, and disappointments in life, is your ability to be resilient. Resilience determines who will win or fail and who will succeed in life.

Researchers have devised a number of strategies for enhancing resiliency, which include physical exercise and maintaining a close social network. Two approaches that have received increasing support for enhancing resiliency are cognitive restructuring techniques and mindfulness mediation.[14]

In this chapter, I introduced you to the concepts of reframing and load shedding as cognitive restructuring techniques to help you better cope with stress and emotions such as fear, disappointment, sadness, and anxiety. Throughout the remainder of this book, I will reinforce this cognitive appraisal method.

In Chapters 4 and 5, I will introduce you to the Law of Resistance, the Law of Motivation, and the Law of Attraction, as well as other principles that will provide meaning to the statement, "Get what you want by changing inwardly."

In Chapters 6 and 7, you will learn proven Cognitive Behavioral Therapy restructuring techniques that will challenge your negative, self-defeating thoughts. The techniques will not only enhance your resiliency to cope with stress, but will also empower you to take control of your emotional and personal life.

Prescription for Success

Nothing worthwhile is easy. I can only provide you with a blueprint that, if you follow it, will change your life. The journey involves a combination of the latest research and practical application in the clinical setting. In my work, I use these proven methods of empowerment to help others take control of their lives, achieve their goals, and enjoy a fulfilling life.

But I can only plant the seeds. It is your responsibility to water and further nourish them. That is why it's so important, in addition to reading this book, to make a commitment to practice the prescribed mental exercises on a daily basis. Use your journal to keep track of what you want and what are doing to achieve it. Your mind is no different from your body — it needs exercise to grow and develop. If you stay focused on what you want, you can develop a mindset programmed for success.

Solution Summary

- Your thoughts have physical properties that affect your life.
- It has been scientifically proven that your thoughts make chemicals that affect your life and actually change your body chemistry.
- You actually feel what you think.
- Sad, angry, or negative thinking can weaken your immune system and contribute to coronary heart disease, ulcers, headaches, depression, and anxiety.
- Happiness is a physical state that the brain can deliberately induce.
- Negative emotions such as fear, despair, and anger help you survive, while positive emotions such as curiosity, joy, and gratitude let you thrive.
- Reduce stress by load shedding.
- Resiliency is the ability to manage your reaction to stress. It can be built up by cognitive restructuring techniques, physical exercise, and close social networking.
- By utilizing the cognitive restructuring technique of reframing, you can change a stressful situation from a threat to a challenge.
- The more you practice reframing stressors into challenges, the better you will get at doing it.

4. Change Thoughts of Resistance and End the Resistance

Change the thought(s) that creates the resistance and there is no more resistance.

— *Robert Conklin*

When I first read this statement, I was captivated by its meaning. In essence, the goal of most psychotherapy and counseling is to help clients transform their lives. Your thoughts determine your existence. Change the thoughts from depression to happiness, from anxiety to calmness, and from conflicts in relationships to tranquility. Worry, fear, and anxiety do not exist in the physical world. It's not the external world that is disabling you; it's your perception of the world that disables you.

I have counseled scores of people who basically think, "I'm not worthy of happiness" and "I'm no good and I don't deserve love." Quite often this crippling thinking stems from family-of-origin issues, especially going back to the formative years between ages one and six years of age. The formative years are like the foundation of a house. If the foundation is unstable, the house will be unstable. As I outlined in my first book, *Relationship Sabotage: Unconscious Factors That Destroy Couples, Marriage and Family*, we learn to trust or not trust by the age of one and a half years, autonomy versus self-doubt by the age of three years, and feeling competent or inferior by the age of six years. During these early childhood years our personality is basically molded by our upbringing. How our parents respond to our needs has a tremendous impact on our maturational process. For example, an infant is completely helpless and dependent on the parents and caregivers to meet its basic needs, such as hunger, thirst, other bodily needs, and emotional needs. If the caregivers meet the infant's basic biological and emotional needs, the child develops an optimistic and trusting perception of the world. However, if the child's basic needs at this stage are neglected, a more pessimistic, distrusting view of the world may result. In Chapter 7 you will learn more about how and why our first six years impact our personality.

Nevertheless, how you learned your faulty way of thinking is less important than the fact that you have within you the power to radically change your life by changing how you think!

Law of Resistance

If you place a grasshopper in a jar and close the lid, you can learn a powerful lesson about human behavior. In this kind of captivity, grasshoppers behave as many people do throughout their lives. At first, the imprisoned grasshopper tries desperately to escape from the jar, using his powerful hind legs to launch his body up against the lid. He tries and tries, and then he tries again. Initially he is very persistent. He may try to get out of the trap for several hours. When he finally stops, however, his trying days are over. He will never again try to escape from the jar by jumping. You could take the lid off of the jar and have a pet grasshopper for life. Once a grasshopper believes that he cannot change his situation, that's it — he stops trying.

In a similar way, once an elephant learns something, it stays with him for life. Many circus elephants are trained as babies to stay in one place by placing a strong chain around one ankle. Like the grasshopper, they initially struggle and struggle to get free until they cannot struggle any more. Once they stop struggling, they will never again try to break loose from something holding them by the ankle. Powerful adult elephants can be held in place by just a thin rope around one of their legs. It has been reported that elephants have burned to death in circus fires when the huge beasts were tethered by small, easily broken ropes.

It is easy to see the parallel between grasshoppers, elephants, and people who are stuck in negative behavior patterns. Once they believe they are defeated and cannot do things to change their situation, they stop trying — they give up and never try again. Even if the lid is removed from their traps, it doesn't occur to them to leave. Even if success or happiness is within their grasp, they are unable to reach out and grab it.

They remain stuck. This is what I call the Law of Resistance. Thoughts that are ingrained through repeated failures *resist* being changed.

You are not a grasshopper, an elephant, or, for that matter, any other lower form of life. You are a human being, the highest form of life ever known. You are separated from lower life forms by your ability to think and reason — and most importantly, by the ability to adapt and change as your environment changes. Adaptability is the reason human beings, despite being smaller and weaker than many animal species, have come to rule the world. You are not a grasshopper; you can change old ways if you follow the simple guidelines outlined in this book.

The Law of Resistance says that your thoughts can be like chains that shackle you to a life of despair, depression, and anxiety. Your thoughts can shackle you to stay in a toxic relationship, not take charge of your children, or not have the ability to create a happier marriage. However, if you understand the Law of Resistance, you realize that the situation *can be changed.* You have the ability to change the very thoughts that are keeping you stuck.

One of my clients broke down sobbing during the initial stage of counseling and actually said, "My thoughts have become obstacles to me. I put up walls so I can't succeed." He was coming to the realization that his self-defeating way of thinking was literally holding him back in a life of misery, worry, and unhappiness.

> It is our thoughts that determine the quality of our existence. If you believe that life is a struggle or something to be endured, then that is exactly how your life will be. However, viewing your life as a giant adventure enhances what you encounter on a daily basis. Take control of those habitual thoughts that occupy your mind. The power to create or destroy is contained within them.
>
> — *Maria Reyes-McDavis*

You create your own life and existence by your way of thinking. If you believe that life is meant to be a struggle, as many do who strive for perfection, life will be a struggle — a life filled with needless worry and anxiety.

Fear of Failure

What would you do if you weren't afraid?
                                                    — *Spencer Johnson*

What a great question! Think about it — how many times do our fear of failure and other negative, crippling fears, hold us hostage? It's amazing how many negative feelings are created by our self-defeating thoughts. Often people are literally immobilized by feelings of despair caused by fear of failure.

When I was going for my doctorate, the university policy decreed that if you had to do two rewrites on a research paper, you were terminated from the program. On one of my papers I received a notice for a rewrite, meaning that I could have been terminated if the rewrite wasn't accepted — all that work would be for naught. I can still remember being immobilized by fear. I often found myself driving around the neighborhood restlessly going for coffee. Eventually I talked my way out of the fear, and my rewrite was accepted. I have seen numerous talented clients too terrified to strive for something they very much want, for fear of failure.

A fear of failure that therapists frequently encounter stems from perfectionism.

> You can say that perfectionism is a crime against humanity. Adaptability is the characteristic that enables the species to survive and if there's one thing perfectionism does, it rigidifies behavior.
> — *Dr. Hara Estroff Marano, psychologist*

Too often, I find myself counseling high school and even middle school students who are overwhelmed with worry because of perfectionism. These students become focused on their performance and fear of making mistakes. They are absorbed in endless self-evaluation. They tend to perceive mistakes as being equivalent to failure. These tormented youngsters often tell me that if they err academically, they will lose the respect of others, especially their parents.

It's no wonder so many of these children eventually are medicated for depression and anxiety. Tragically, they lose their childhood because their lives are preoccupied with thinking about and trying to defeat criticism from critical and over-demanding parents. Perfectionism is not genetic; it is learned at an early age — the result of parents who love their child conditionally. Conditional love means that parental approval is not given unless the child meets the parents' standards for perfection. If the child achieves the established goal, the parents grant approval. If not, the child is criticized. Conditional love also serves to enhance the parents' sense of self-worth at the expense of the child.

Ironically, striving for perfection becomes an unconsciously self-defeating way for the child to avoid feelings of inadequacy and criticism. Truly striving for perfection is delusional because it can never be achieved — the child is doomed to a life of feeling inadequate. Many perfectionists procrastinate about starting tasks because they fear making mistakes and, as you can clearly see, if you don't start, you can't fail.

> A life spent making mistakes is not only more
> memorable, but more useful than a life spent doing
> nothing.
>
> — *George Bernard Shaw*

Again, what would you do if you weren't afraid? What would you do if it was all right to make mistakes? If you make a mistake, what's the worst that could happen? We all make mistakes and hopefully we can learn from them. How many people never achieve their potential academically, socially, or career-wise, because they fear making a mistake or feeling foolish? How many times have you lost out on an opportunity because of fear? Later in this book I will fully explore with you the *should haves, could haves,* and *would haves* that only add to the fear of making future mistakes.

Law of Motivation

The optimum level of motivation decreases with
increasing task difficulty.
             — Dr. Robert Yerkes and Dr. John Dodson,
                            psychologists and researchers

Your perception of a task determines your motivation or drive to accomplish your goal. For example, if you feel that you can succeed at taking college or vocational school courses, you are highly motivated to succeed. Conversely, if you feel you will fail, you will fail. How we think determines our existence and our failures.

For years I have consciously kept the Law of Motivation (also known in the literature as the Yerkes-Dodson Law) in mind and utilized its principles, especially when the task at hand appears daunting. I devised plans to break down the task into smaller, more manageable parts. Such an action provides momentum that magnetically attracts me to accomplish the goal. It will do the same for you.

> Take a moment, reflect back on your life, and think about missed opportunities to improve your life. Missed because you thought too little of your abilities. Missed because the goal(s) you wanted to accomplish appeared overwhelming. The operative word here is *appeared*. Write down the top three that you think of today.

You view the world through your old glasses, and often they are cloudy — your habitual way of thinking often limits your ability to see clearly.

How you look at a situation is very important, for how
you think about a problem may defeat you before you

ever do anything about it. When you get discouraged or
depressed, try changing your attitude from negative to
positive and see how life can change for you.
Remember, your attitude toward a situation can help
you to change it – you create the very atmosphere for
defeat or victory.

— *Franco Harris*

You create the very atmosphere for defeat or victory. You can take
the first step towards conquering the grasshopper's problem with the
Law of Resistance and change old, dysfunctional, habitual ways of
thinking. You can create a new self. The self is not something we find, it
is something that we create.

Too many people focus on what they fear or what they want to avoid.
Focus on what you want. When you stay focused on what you want, your
motivation will continue to drive you to reach your dreams. Success
breeds success — you'll be open and receptive to discover ways to
achieve what you want, leaving the grasshopper mentality behind. When
you start to control your thinking, you become empowered to take more
control of your life.

There are lots of reasons for controlling your thinking.
Perhaps one of the most important reasons is that your
thoughts create your feelings. If you focus on the bright
side of things or look to opportunity or how to make the
most of whatever happens to you, then you can
improve how you feel on a regular basis. Think of it as
feeling good by design. By mastering your thoughts you
can master your feelings.

— *Dr. David Burns, psychiatrist and author*

A simple daily exercise that will help you start looking on the bright
side of life is when you wake up in the morning, reflect for a moment,
and decide for yourself that today, on a scale of one to ten, will be an
eight, nine, or ten day. Decide that the day will be enjoyable, then work
to make it true. During the day, do one or two things that make you feel

good, and stay in the moment. If you are feeling good, you are creating a path in line with your decisions. If you are feeling bad, what path do you think you are on?

When you start to view life as more exciting and become more positive about life on a daily basis, you will magnetically attract and perpetuate a healthier and happier state of well-being.

The Impact of Negative Self-talk

> Watch your thoughts because they become words.
> Watch your words because they become actions. Watch
> your actions because they become habits. Watch your
> habits for they will become character, which will
> become your destiny.
>
> *— Lao Tzu*

Our thoughts determine how we feel, which in turn determines our behavior. As I said earlier in this chapter, too many clients, especially young clients, think, "If I fail, I'm a loser." Such thinking makes them feel anxious and depressed. These feelings are reflected either in behaviorally trying for perfection at any cost or feeling helplessly stuck. Eventually this scenario becomes habitual and defines their state of being, their character.

In Chapter 6 you will be introduced to specific, proven ways to challenge and change your faulty, distorted thinking. For now, I would like you to practice uncovering negative self-talk. As you learned in Chapter 3, negative thoughts actually have physical effects that cause your brain to become anxious and depressed. In the following section you can become consciously aware of your habitual, negative self-talk.

Uncovering Self-Defeating Emotions

When I ask my clients to write down their negative thoughts, they often reply, "My thoughts are fleeting." "I don't know what I am thinking." "I can't possibly keep track of my negative thoughts." My response to these statements is simple and, for many people, powerful. Our thoughts determine *how we feel*. How you are feeling emotionally at a given moment is a direct reflection of what you are thinking. Behind every emotion is a thought.

Take a few minutes and reflect on the following situations: Death of a close family member — you are probably feeling sad. A time when someone insulted you — you probably feel hurt or angry. When your spouse doesn't hear what you are saying — you probably feel frustrated or discounted. And last, take a few minutes and think about the first time you fell in love. Again, our feelings or emotional state at a given moment are a direct reflection of our thoughts.

> When you feel sad, anxious, hurt, or frustrated, grab a notepad and jot down what you are thinking. This will enlighten you about why you are feeling depressed, anxious, hurt, frustrated, etc.

By writing down your negative, self-defeating thoughts you are taking the first step to gain control of your life. When you note your faulty thoughts, you are on your way to change the thoughts that create the resistance, so there is no more resistance to hold you back from experiencing all that life has to offer.

SOLUTION SUMMARY

- Law of Resistance: Change the thought(s) that cause the resistance and there is no more resistance to a happier, peaceful life.
- Avoid the grasshopper mentality — you have the ability to change and create a healthy, fulfilling life.
- Your thoughts create your existence.
- Law of Motivation: The optimum level of motivation decreases with increasing task difficulty.
- Your thoughts determine how you feel. Behind every emotion is a thought.
- How you are feeling emotionally is a direct reflection of what you are thinking.

• Writing down your negative thoughts is the first step to changing them.

5. Get What You Want by Changing Inwardly

Thus far, I have presented the Law of Resistance — change the thought(s) that cause the resistance and there is no more resistance; the Law of Association — like thoughts attract like thoughts; and the Law of Motivation — the optimum level of motivation decreases with increasing task difficulty.

Law of Attraction

The fourth pivotal law is the Law of Attraction, which says that a positive attitude and a positive way of living attract more positive, good things into your life.

> I have found that if you love life, life will love you back.
> — Arthur Robinstein

How true! In my professional experience, I see firsthand the Law of Attraction in action, its magnetic effect on people's lives.

Eric entered counseling because his life was falling apart. At age thirty-two, Eric was single and in management at a major financial institution. His symptoms included feelings of sadness, insomnia, social isolation, guilt, and failure. He had also been passed up for a promotion. Obviously he was depressed, and I taught him the principles and laws outlined in this book. As Eric started to feel better, good things started to happen to him. The better he felt, the more he attracted good things, not only professionally but also personally. Due to his new state of mind, he was able to attract a girlfriend and he was more productive at work.

Only a few weeks prior to therapy, his life felt hopeless and he was in a state of despair. He viewed himself and the world through dark-tinted glasses, a world filled with doom and gloom. In his depressed state, he was unknowingly placed by the Law of Attraction in a self-defeating, self-deprecating lens. For him, the Law of Attraction was acting like a magnet — his dismal state of mind was attracting bad things into his life, which naturally attracted more bad things, which led to problems with his social, personal, and career life. His life was spiraling out of control.

The Nature of Feelings

Our feelings are mirrors to our state of mind and mental well-being.

— *Dr. David Burns, psychiatrist and author*

Our feelings are a direct reflection of our thoughts. I always ask my depressed or anxious clients, "What are you thinking?" When my clients feel sad and hopeless, they are thinking things, such as "I'm no good." "I can't do anything right." or "I'm a loser." Thus they feel hopeless and helpless. Conversely, when they feel joy, enthusiasm, and happiness, they naturally feel good about themselves and they attract more good things into their lives. Eric's distorted, negative thought process determined his emotional state, a state of despair and hopelessness.

Like Eric, many people feel that they have little or no control over their emotional state. It is what it is. What a pity! No wonder their emotional state bounces around like a piece of paper blown by the wind. No wonder they feel their life is out of control. No wonder that they feel helpless and anxious. No wonder they resort to medication to try to function. These people believe that their emotional well-being is determined by forces outside of themselves, but they are wrong. The key is really within.

Just because you feel a certain way doesn't make it a reality. Just because you feel guilty doesn't mean you deserve to feel that way. Again, your emotional state is a reflection of how you think. I see too many single parents who feel guilty about raising their child or children alone because the father or mother deserted the family. These nurturing and loving people should not have feelings of guilt; they should feel good because they are caring, responsible parents.

To Know What You Are Thinking;
Ask Yourself, "What Am I Feeling?"

Most of my clients initially don't believe that they can master their emotional state. When I say that their thoughts are what lead to their feelings, they tell me that they aren't even aware of their thoughts. I reply that you can be aware of your thinking by noticing how you feel at a given moment. The two are tied together. Undoubtedly, if you are feeling bad, you are thinking bad thoughts. But thoughts are not always correct. Just because you think it, doesn't make it so. Just because you think you should feel guilty as a single parent, doesn't mean in reality you are doing a poor job. But, sure as can be, if you do think you should feel guilty, that's how you will feel.

Our feelings are a reflection of our thoughts. In Chapter 4, I asked that you start to be aware of your thoughts. I am now requesting that you start keeping a record of your thoughts journal. Make a deliberate effort to record your thoughts via your feelings.

As you read this book, you will come to appreciate the necessity of such journal activity to master your emotional state and have the tools to take control of your life and your future.

Celebrate the Good Feelings

I tell my clients that basically you have two categories of feelings: good and bad. You know the feelings that make you feel bad — fear, disappointment, guilt, anger, and resentment. These are the feelings or emotions that put you into survival mode. When you feel bad, you attract more bad things to your life. You also know the feelings that make you feel good — joy, hope, triumph, happiness, curiosity, and gratitude.

When you celebrate the good feelings, you not only feel good, you naturally attract more good things to yourself.

It's impossible to have bad feelings if you have good thoughts. Think about it. Take a moment and reflect upon a positive experience such as receiving a compliment, accomplishing a goal, or taking a pleasant holiday. It's impossible to have bad feelings if you have good thoughts. Good thinking makes you feel good.[15]

The four laws work in conjunction to change and improve your life. When you celebrate good feelings, you are negating bad feelings (Law of Resistance). When you are feeling good, you attract more good thoughts (Law of Association). Your optimistic and positive approach to life attracts more good things into your life (Law of Attraction). Success breeds success, and you will become highly motivated to sustain your new way of living to realize your goals (Law of Motivation).

Focus on What You Want

Our thoughts and feelings ultimately determine our present and future. As I said in Chapter 3, our thoughts can literally harm us both mentally and physically. Our thoughts and emotions determine our success and whether or not we achieve our goals. Those thoughts and emotions reflect our ability to cope with stress and find happiness. Our thoughts and emotions are crucial to our success in dealing with depression, anxiety, relationships, careers, marriage, and the ability to effectively rear our children.

When you focus on what you want, you'll find a way to be successful. When you focus on what you fear, what you want to avoid, or what makes you anxious, you won't find a way to be successful.

For example, when I was a young man, I worked for a major corporation. At that stage in my life I was not a therapist. I was promoted to a position in Minneapolis. My pregnant wife, Alexia, and I moved from the East Coast to the Twin Cities area in February. In addition to the pressure I felt of learning a new position, my wife of almost two years had to buy our first home during the freezing, dark days of winter. This was our first time away from home. We were both scared because our lives were changing so dramatically. Naturally, just starting out as a married couple, our funds were limited, so I asked my father for a loan of $3,000 for a down payment on a house in Burnsville, Minnesota. His response was that he couldn't lend me the money because it was all tied up in mutual funds. What a rude awakening! I was faced with the stark reality that I was on my own. My pregnant wife was unable to assist us financially.

As I reflect back on those times, I see that I focused on what I feared: doing a poor job and making mistakes, especially at work. I was also consumed by fears and anxieties about the responsibility of being a father. These fears and anxieties only served to further inhibit my performance at work. On top of all that, the person who was supposed to train me in my new position as manager of training suddenly died the first week after we arrived. This reinforced and perpetuated my fear of failing. Remember, when you focus on what you fear or want to avoid, you won't be successful. After about eighteen months, I was terminated. It did not have to be that way. If I knew then what I know now, if I had focused on what I wanted, I would have empowered myself to be successful and confident.

My thinking focused on failing and ways to fail. To others in the corporation, I appeared insecure and incompetent. In the context of the Four Laws — the Law of Resistance, the Law of Association, the Law of Motivation, and the Law of Attraction — I was destined to fail.

My central thoughts revolved around failing (Law of Resistance — change the thought that is causing the resistance). These thoughts created my reality of incompetence, insecurity, and gloom. Remember, like thoughts attract like thoughts (Law of Association). My thinking naturally spiraled down. My thought processes were "What if my boss discovers I'm a fraud? If he realizes that I'm a fraud, how will I support my family? I'll never find another job, and how will we ever get back to family on the East Coast?" In my mind, my goals were unattainable (Law of Motivation — success breeds success). Consequently, in this foggy state of mind, I projected incompetence towards my supervisor and colleagues (Law of Attraction). My thoughts surely determined my existence: a state of insecurity and depression. Last, in addition to being depressed, I was anxious to the point of having panic attacks. I feared giving presentations to the point of relying on the anti-anxiety medication Xanax as a crutch. I was relying on something outside myself to function.

As you will learn in Chapter 6, you can train yourself to refute negative, self-defeating thoughts. Today, I carefully select my thoughts. I will not allow myself to be depressed or anxious to the point of having panic attacks. I have learned, as you will, to focus on what I want, celebrate the good feelings, and be grateful for all life has to offer.

People Find More Ways to Make Themselves Feel Miserable

In my work I often encounter people who resist feeling good about themselves. That sounds ridiculous, but it's true. When they start to feel good about themselves, they literally don't feel comfortable, and they tend to revert back to their comfortable, familiar state of despair, depression, or anxiety. As they start to feel good, they often wait for the other shoe to drop. Often such people come from a chaotic, dysfunctional, or alcoholic family where they experienced little control in their lives, and the shoe often did drop. As adults, they tend to need to be in control of all aspects of their life —a fruitless goal that only further perpetuates anxiety or the need to control things that can't be controlled.

Change is difficult, and people resist change mostly because of fear: fear of the unknown, the unfamiliar. In my work I illustrate how people resist positive, good, healthy feelings and change. For example, even a positive change, such as when one alcoholic spouse stops drinking, is difficult.

I saw this in the Tooly family: Mr. Tooly drank for 20 of his 22 years of marriage. It was not until Mr. Tooly stopped drinking and went to counseling and Alcoholics Anonymous that Mrs. Tooly threatened divorce. What happens in so many alcoholic families is that the disease is insidious and gradually infects the whole family. Mrs. Tooly had assumed responsibility for the family. She took the kids to their sporting events, paid the bills, made excuses for her husband's absences, and so forth. In other words, she had to take on a lot of responsibility and had assumed control over family matters. Once Mr. Tooly became sober and more aware of family matters, he wanted to become more involved and have more control. His positive change disrupted the balance and caused surprisingly high levels of anxiety in his wife, which almost led to divorce.

Usually, due to family-of-origin issues, people feel that they don't deserve love. For example: "If my parents didn't love me, why should anyone else or even I love myself?" "I'm not worthy of being loved." In my work I see people who start to feel better, then focus on and keep waiting for the other shoe to drop, and when it sometimes does, they say, "You see, I'll never win, I'll never be happy." Still others are anxious and say, "If I let my guard down, if I'm not hypervigilant, something bad will happen." I have my clients familiarize themselves with the laws and blueprint in this book. Once they use this information, they change for the better. They change to varying degrees, but their change is positive and rewarding. They let go of the grasshopper mentality.

For deep-seated family-of-origin issues, long-term psychoanalysis is clearly the therapy of the past. Today, therapists utilize the principles described in this book, specifically those in Chapters 6 and 7, and successfully refute negative thoughts carried from childhood which sabotage efforts to achieve a better way of living.

Finding Purpose in Your Life

Without purpose our life is meaningless.

— *Anonymous*

I tell my clients, especially the adolescents, that they need a purpose in their lives. Without goals, we are like a rudderless ship in the ocean, drifting aimlessly on a course to nowhere! Recent studies show that truly happy people understand that sustained happiness is not solely about doing things you like; it also requires growth and expansion of your comfort zone to become curious about what the future may hold. Happy people tend not to view the future as a threat or something to fear, but as an adventure, an opportunity, or a challenge that can be accomplished. They transform or reframe the unknown of the future into an eager curiosity about the future.[16]

According to a 2013 study[17], curiosity and search activity simply feel good. Certain reward-related neurotransmitters in your brain are increased when you pursue a specific goal. The more you have of them, the better you feel. This fact explains why shopping for something is often more fun than the actual purchase, and why so many people get addicted to gambling. Happy and curious people, even though they have long-term goals, are more able to savor the moment, and are grateful for life on a daily basis.

Gratitude

What you can do right now to begin to turn your life around is to start making a list of things for which you are grateful. This will rechannel your energy and start to change the way you think. This exercise can be a powerful initial step in focusing your fears, complaints, and problems in a different, positive direction. You will start to be grateful for all the things you feel good about.

Gratitude is one of the thriving emotions. By feeling grateful for even the small things we all take for granted, we start to appreciate and embrace our lives and we tend to focus on the good and enjoyable aspects of our lives. Literally, we are physically rewiring our brain to focus on the thriving emotions and not the survival emotions. All too often we take an aspect of our life for granted until we lose it. Some of the endless examples are our mobility, our eyesight, our sense of smell, our health, our spouse, our children, and our pets. Incidentally, the major reason why women seek divorce is lack of validation, being taken for granted by their spouses.

> Gratitude has produced the most purely joyful moments
> that have been known to man.
>
> — *G. K. Chesterton*

Please don't take this seemingly simple concept for granted. Being grateful can dramatically change your life, improve your marriage, and effectively deal with depression. As soon as you start to feel differently about what you already have, you will start to attract more good things. It is impossible to bring more into your life if you are not grateful for what you have, because your dominant thoughts and feelings are focused on negative emotions. Focusing on negative emotions, such as jealousy, resentment, hate, and disgust, cannot bring you what you want. Such thinking will propel you back to what you don't want, and you surely don't want that! When you take the time to be grateful for what you have, you are also regulating your emotional state, resetting it in a healthy way.

Practice shifting your focus from what you don't have, such as a bigger home, new car, and perfect health, to what you are grateful for in your life. Make a conscious effort to enjoy the daily things that you currently take for granted. Start by enjoying a hot shower, savoring a cup of coffee, greeting your spouse and children, exercising in the morning, or saying grace before a meal. Here's a way to celebrate what you are grateful for.

Keep a log and write down three positive things that happen each day.

This will help to convince you that favorable outcomes actually do happen, and that continuing this practice will make positive changes in how you view and approach life. You will start to feel good, and feeling good attracts more things that make you feel good. By being grateful, you will see your life and your health as gifts and take measures to cherish them.

I would also like you to write down something that upsets you each day as practice for changing your thoughts.

Each day write down one thing that upsets you. Then try to brainstorm: How might this be a blessing in disguise? How could I reframe this event and turn it to my advantage? What is good about this? Write down your insights.

With practice you will learn to transform potentially threatening stressors into challenges that you have the ability to control. Feeling good will naturally attract more good things that make you feel good.

Savor the Moment

> Only as I am aware of the present will I have the
> opportunity to be fully alive.
>
> — *Ann Wilson Schoel*

Another characteristic of happy people is that they have the ability to live in the moment. Learning to live in the moment frees you from ruminating about failures in the past and anxieties for the future. In this stage in your journey to attract good things in your life, start by embracing life, moment by moment. I will expand upon living in the moment in Chapter 7, but for now I just want to introduce you to this psychologically sound principle that, combined with gratitude, becomes a powerful impetus to help you start to see life in a new way.

As I mentioned earlier, having a purpose in life or having a long-term goal is motivating and uplifting, but we need to keep sight of the importance of savoring the moment. Too often I see students whose only goal is to acquire a degree, thus they neglect to enjoy and fully participate in the process of learning. Unfortunately, since their only goal is to complete school, they overlook daily enjoyment during the process.

At times I find myself rushing to write, and when I find myself doing so, I refocus on the pleasure I gain from the process of writing. Taking the time to enjoy the process allows me to become more creative, and hopefully more inspirational.

Activate Your Emotional Reset Button

You can view the ability to shift your emotions from bad to good as if you were dealing cards. In this case, it's not cheating to stack your emotional deck to help assure that you stay on top emotionally and are able to better take control of your life. There is no opponent you are trying to defeat. There's only you.

You may find that thinking of your ability to refocus on good things is a kind of reset button. Life naturally has its ups and downs. Again, the downs can serve you as a contrast, a frame of reference, and enable you to better appreciate the ups, the good things. When you mentally activate the reset button, you activate focusing on the good feelings. When you go down, you know you can switch your focus from bad to good things by the flick of a switch. With practice you can relearn or become reconditioned to make this positive emotional shift.

Here are a few of the ways we have talked about that will help you emotionally shift or refocus from bad to good feelings: reframing the event, viewing the situation or event as a challenge and not a threat, being grateful, and savoring the moment. Other ways to emotionally shift or refocus to more pleasant feelings are listening to music, watching a funny movie, and thinking of a beautiful mountain or ocean scene.

Boulders, Rocks, and Pebbles

Many of my clients have discovered that the *Boulders, Rocks, and Pebbles* analogy is helpful in reframing life's daily aggravations and stressors. Although it is a simple concept, it can provide you with a mechanism to cope with stress more manageably. This analogy will help you to overcome feelings of being overwhelmed and hopeless.

Boulders exemplify critical life incidents that seriously impact your life, such as death of a loved one, a diagnosis of cancer, or destruction of your home by a tornado.

Rocks represent minor setbacks and disruptions in your life, such as not receiving a promotion, a car accident, or a temporary illness.

Pebbles represent upsetting but minor events, such as a flat tire, an altercation with a co-worker, or being late for an event.

If you label a negative event with the size of the stone, it will help you to keep things in perspective. It's all right to be blown away for a while by boulders and to ask for help in moving them out of your way. However, if it's just a pebble, pick it up, toss it to the side of the road, and move on. Some things just aren't as important as others, and realizing that makes it easier to know when you can shift your thoughts to positive ones.

> Life is a mirror and will reflect back to the thinker what
> s/he thinks into it.
> — *Ernest Holmes, American writer and philosopher*

You get what you want by changing inwardly. You get what you want out of life by celebrating good feelings. When you feel good, you attract more good things to yourself, and you tend to get what you want out of life. In other words, you get out of life what you put into it. Focus on what you want. Your thoughts and feelings ultimately determine how you live in the present and in the future.

You can learn to better master your emotional state, to activate your reset button. Once you learn to master your emotions and thoughts, you have the means to create your own reality and destiny. As a result, more good things will come to you. Not only will you become more in control of your world, you will also develop more confidence and project an aura of optimism.

Solution Summary

- The Law of Attraction: Like a magnet, a positive attitude and lifestyle attracts more good things in your life.
- Get what you want by changing inwardly.
- Celebrating good feelings is important.
- Focus on what you want, not on what you fear or want to avoid.
- People can find ways to make themselves feel miserable or ways to make themselves feel happy and content.
- There is power in gratitude.
- Savor the moment.
- You can activate your emotional-reset button.
- Boulders, Rocks, and Pebbles can help you keep perspective in your life.

6. A Clinically Proven Method to Empower Change

> People do not want to be anxious or depressed but don't know how to implement change.
>
> — *Dr. William Matta*

My anxious or depressed clients start counseling because they feel miserable and they don't know how to alleviate the horrible feelings they endure. How often have you heard the statement, "think positive"? That advice sounds good, but when confronted with the harsh realities of life, people tend to fold under pressure. This is especially true for my depressed or anxious clients. They aspire to possess a mental state of well-being, but lack the means to get there. They too easily resort to medication to address the symptoms of depression or anxiety, but they fail to understand the relationship between their dysfunctional thinking and their depression or anxiety. In essence, they feel that their mental well-being is out of their control and can only be controlled by medications or something outside of themselves to make them feel better. Of course, medications do serve a definite purpose, but in my opinion many people rely too heavily on medication, and not enough on their own potential to control their mental state.

> Psychological problems...may result from commonplace processes such as faulty learning, making incorrect references on the basis of inadequate or incorrect information, and not distinguishing adequately between imagination and reality. Moreover, thinking can be

> unrealistic because it is derived from erroneous
> premises...The formula for treatment may be stated in
> simple terms: The therapist helps the patient to identify
> his warped thinking and to learn more realistic ways to
> formulate his experiences.
> — *Dr. Aaron Beck, psychiatrist and author*

Thoughts are interpretations of our perceptions of the world. Just because an external situation or event causes you distress does not mean it has to be that way. It's not the external object or situation that necessarily causes distress, it's our perception of it that causes the pain. Thoughts are not direct results of reality. They are reflections of your reality, how you perceive the world. Your thoughts or schemas of the world determine how you feel and your behavior — and further determine your feelings and behavior in the future.

Brody was only 18 years old when he entered counseling. Prior to starting therapy, he spent 21 days in an inpatient mental health facility for depression. Specifically, he felt hopeless and helpless, primarily because he felt that he had no future. As a senior in high school, he was not motivated to study, even though he was highly intelligent. His grades were poor, and he had no idea what he wanted to do in the future. He had low self-esteem, was indecisive, lacked confidence, and was depressed. Obviously his view of the world was tainted with doom and gloom. Without counseling, his schema of the world at the present time and in the future would never change. He would tend to continue to focus on the bad things in life and naturally attract more bad things.

Clients who suffer from anxiety disorders follow a pattern similar to those with depression. For them, it's not the external object or situation that causes the survival emotions to be activated; it's their schema or thoughts about the event that causes the anxious reaction, the going into survival mode. People suffering from anxiety, including panic attacks, greatly overestimate or magnify the severity of the so-called threat, becoming overwhelmed and unable to cope with the situation. As you learned in Chapter 3, they see the event as a threat, not a challenge that can be resolved. Anxiety-ridden people and depressed people feel and behave as if they are trapped — as they should, because they are trapped. The trap is their repeatedly self-sabotaging way of thinking, a way of thinking that dominates their life in the present and will determine what they attract for themselves in the future.

> I am convinced that a person's behavior springs from one's ideas.
>
> — *Dr. Alfred Adler, psychiatrist and author*

I have been an adjunct college professor of psychology for over thirty years. When I teach about the history of psychology, my students learn about one of the great pioneers in the field of psychology, Dr. Alfred Adler (1870-1937). If you get the opportunity, read about his teachings and what he calls individual psychology. His work is the precursor for cognitive restructuring, the concept that we are influenced not by facts but by our interpretation of the facts.

In the 1960s, Dr. Aaron Beck further developed cognitive restructuring techniques based upon the premise that irrational thoughts were the major causes for depression, anxiety, and panic attacks. Dr. Beck's work has emerged as a therapeutic method that has been proven to be more effective for most people's depression and anxiety than medication, and without potentially dangerous side effects.

Irrational Thoughts Equal Mental Disorders

Your initial impression of this statement, "Irrational thoughts equal mental disorders," may be, "So what? Everybody has irrational thoughts, but everybody doesn't have mental disorders." Yes, at times everybody has irrational thoughts, such as "I'm no good." "I can't do anything right." "I have to be perfect." "Things never go right for me." or "I failed." But for many people such thoughts are fleeting or quickly interpreted as untrue. The intensity and frequency of such thoughts also can make a difference. Everyone, even the most mentally healthy and successful people, will temporarily entertain irrational thinking, but healthy people don't allow such thinking to become a way of living.

For others, irrational, self-deprecating thinking permeates every aspect of their lives. Such self-defeating thinking directly causes a poor self-image, poor self-worth, and feelings of despair. Negative self-talk further afflicts every aspect of their lives — themselves, their relationships, their career choices, and their marital and financial status.

Others have been conditioned for years to think irrational thoughts because of a dysfunctional childhood upbringing.

Erickson's Developmental Stages

Depending on how we were raised, especially during the first six years, we learn trust versus mistrust; autonomy versus self-doubt; initiative versus guilt; and feeling competent versus feeling inferior.

During the first stage, from birth to about one and one-half years of age, we learn to trust or not trust depending on our caretaker's behavior. During this stage the baby is completely helpless and dependent on the parent(s) to meet the child's basic needs. If the caregivers meet the baby's basic biological and emotional needs, the child develops an optimistic and trusting perception of the world. Conversely, if a child's basic need for food, fluids, diaper changes, and comforting are neglected at this stage, a more pessimistic and distrusting view of the world may result.

In the second stage, autonomy versus shame unfolds during the second and third years of the child's life. During this time, parents begin to lead the child to taking more responsibility for himself. The child starts to feed and dress himself as well as to master toileting. If all goes well, the child develops a sense of self-sufficiency. However, if the parents are too critical or demanding of the child's efforts, the child may develop a sense of personal shame and doubt. As an adult, he may feel anxious, have low self-esteem, feel insecure, and constantly second-guess himself. Frequently, as a result of low self-worth, the person may underestimate his abilities in all aspects of his life, including career, friends, and potential mate. All too often I see teenagers with low self-worth — and they gravitate toward other teens with low self-worth who use drugs to bolster their egos.

Table 3.1. Erikson's Psychological Stages[18]

STAGE ONE: Birth to 1½ years — trust versus mistrust

ADEQUATE RESOLUTION: basic sense of safety
INADEQUATE RESOLUTION: insecurity, anxiety

STAGE TWO: 1½ to 3 years — autonomy versus shame

ADEQUATE RESOLUTION: perception of self as an agent capable of controlling own body and making things happen
INADEQUATE RESOLUTION: feelings of inadequacy to control events

STAGE THREE: 3 to 6 years — initiative versus guilt

ADEQUATE RESOLUTION: Confidence in oneself as initiator, creator
INADEQUATE RESOLUTION: Lack of self-worth

STAGE FOUR: 6 to puberty — industry versus inferiority

ADEQUATE RESOLUTION: Adequacy in basic social and intellectual skills
INADEQUATE RESOLUTION: Lack of self-confidence, feelings of failure

---

The third stage, initiative versus guilt, encompasses ages three through six years. In this stage the child starts to use his imagination and takes initiative for his own behavior. At this stage the child's behavior will sometimes conflict with the rules of the parents. If the parents are over-controlling, the child may develop feelings of guilt and low self-worth. During this stage, parents need to support their child's emerging independence while maintaining appropriate control.

In my experience, this is where parents need to establish mutually agreeable, consistently applied rules with natural, logical consequences. It is crucial that the parents do not undermine each other and that they be consistent. An eye-opening example: A couple recently came into my office, upset because they couldn't control their two boys' bedtime —the boys simply would go to bed when the boys wanted. When I asked the mother the ages of their boys, she replied two years and four years. What we found was that this lack of control reflected serious problems between the husband and wife. The parents' discord and power struggle was reflected in their unwillingness to properly discipline their children.

The fourth stage, industry versus inferiority encompasses age six years through puberty, learning social skills beyond the family setting in realms such as the neighborhood, church, and school. In this stage the child learns the value of achievement and learns to take pride and achieve a sense of competence.

If you would like to read further about these psychological stages, refer to the writings of Erik Erickson.

The good news is that even if you experienced a dysfunctional, chaotic upbringing, you can change your life by changing the way you think. You can start to change your life — right now! — by following this book's blueprint.

Create an Open Mind or Create a Self-fulfilling Prophecy

I challenge you to become open-minded to positive change, or you will be destined for self-fulfilling prophecy. If you take too many precautions for fear of failing, you will fail. When you are not focusing on what you want, you are focusing on failing. You focus on and magnify every small human error that you make — and being human, you will make mistakes.

For example, prior to giving an important presentation, if you focus on "I can't sweat." "I can't project fear." "Don't stutter." "Don't show anxiety." — guess what? You sweat more, your heartbeat escalates, you get nervous, and you start stuttering. Eventually, if you continue to focus on these reactions, your presentation spirals down and the speech is a disaster. Self-fulfilling prophecy comes to fruition. How do you think you'll feel the next time you are called upon to give a speech?

You need to focus on what you want to project to your audience — confidence, enthusiasm, and inspiration. Prior to your presentation, you want to focus, if possible, on past peak experiences, those times when your presentations were great, those times, even if rare, when you gave a speech and you felt on top of the world.

Another example of self-fulfilling prophecy is people whose schemas or thoughts revolve around not feeling good enough. Their basic assumption permeates their whole life. They feel they are not good enough and project these feelings onto others and the world. Unfortunately, their life is dedicated to, and they are looking for, events that seem to reaffirm that they are not good enough. In their social life, they may ignore other peoples' positive gestures and affirmations because they are hypervigilant to signs or triggers that confirm their basic dysfunctional assumptions. It's no wonder that they have the uncanny ability to attract bad things into their lives. If you look for the bad in your life, naturally you will attract more bad things.

> If you don't know where you are going, you'll wind up
> somewhere else.
> — *Dr. Alfred Adler, psychologist and author*

Start to view your thinking as the captain of your ship. The captain controls the ship's course, its actions, and final destinations. It may be helpful to view your feelings as a navigation system, which provides you with feedback and lets you know if you are on course.

The Ten Cognitive Distortions

An empirically proven method to keep on course is to measure and analyze your thoughts against ten common, negative thought distortions in order to uncover your irrational thoughts; replace your faulty, self-defeating thoughts with rational thoughts; and initiate steps to terminate negative behavior and achieve a state of emotional well-being.

As you learn about the ten cognitive distortions, keep in mind that your thoughts affect your feelings and your feelings affect your behavior

— thinking affects feelings affects behavior. If you feel depressed or anxious, you are thinking depressing or anxious thoughts that in turn affect your behavior.

Checklist of Cognitive Distortions[19]

For your convenience as you read through the rest of this book, the Checklist of Cognitive Distortions can also be found in Appendix D.

ALL-OR-NONE THINKING: You look at things in absolute black and white categories.

"I must be perfect or I'm no good." "I must never make a mistake." "I ate a brownie, my diet is ruined." "He's always putting me down."

OVERGENERALIZATION: You view a negative event as a never-ending pattern of defeat.

"I failed statistics in high school; I know I'll fail in college." "Boys jilted me in the past; why bother to try to meet Cal?" "I've read self-help books before for my depression and anxiety; they didn't help."

MENTAL FILTER: You dwell on the negatives and ignore the positives.

"I have good qualities, but the bad parts of me matter more." "I am a good speaker, but I make too many mistakes when I give a speech."

DISCOUNTING THE POSITIVES: You insist that your accomplishments or positive qualities don't count.

"They're just saying I gave a good speech to make me feel good." "Yes, I did get a B+ in the course, but I didn't get an A."

JUMPING TO CONCLUSIONS: There are two ways to jump to conclusions: fortune telling and mind reading. Fortune telling is when you arbitrarily predict that things will turn out badly. Mind

reading is when you assume that people are reacting negatively to you when there's no definite evidence for this.

Fortune telling: "I'll always be depressed; I'll never get better." "I'll mess up on the speech." "He won't give me a raise; I just know it."

Mind reading: "Everyone will see how nervous I look." "I know people don't like me." "He never said it, but I know he doesn't like me."

MAGNIFICATION OR MINIMIZATION: You blow things way out of proportion or you shrink their importance inappropriately.

"What if I never get better?" "What if I make a mistake?" "What if they see I'm nervous?" "So what if I get on the honor role? I'm supposed to be on it." "So what? I gave a great speech. I'm expected to do that."

EMOTIONAL REASONING: You reason from how you feel.

"I feel like an idiot, so I really must be one." "I feel guilty, therefore I must be guilty." "If I feel that I've failed, I must have failed because feelings don't lie." "If I feel this way, it must be real."

***SHOULD* STATEMENTS: You criticize yourself or other people with *shoulds* or *shouldn'ts*. *Musts*, *oughts*, and *have tos* are similar offenders.**

When you tell yourself that you should have, you feel guilty. When you tell someone else that they should have, you feel angry. "I should have been more confident during my speech." "I shouldn't ever (or must never) forgive myself for that mistake." "You should have realized that I was hurting emotionally." "You should know what I want in the marriage by now." The point is that we all make mistakes. It's water under the bridge — just try to learn from your mistake and move on.

LABELING: You identify with statements of shortcoming.

Instead of telling yourself that you made a mistake, you tell yourself, "I'm a loser." "I'm a failure." "I'm no good." "I'm a fool."

PERSONALIZATION AND BLAME: You blame yourself for something you weren't entirely responsible for, or you blame other people and overlook ways that your attitudes and behavior might contribute to a problem.

"It's your fault we are having these marital problems right now." "This wouldn't have happened if you had…" "It's your fault that I…"

Uncovering Your Faulty Thinking

When I ask clients to note their thoughts, they often retort that their thoughts are constantly changing and they'll need a butterfly net to capture them. Some of the methods that I utilize to help them uncover their faulty thinking are identifying feelings, answering questions, and the rebuttal technique.

Identify feelings

You can know what you're thinking by what you are feeling. When you are feeling sad, depressed, anxious, or apprehensive, get in the habit of stopping and noting what you are thinking. Your thoughts are a direct reflection of what you are feeling. If you are feeling anxious, you're thinking anxious thoughts. If you are feeling depressed, you are thinking depressing or hopeless thoughts.

> Continue to keep track of what is happening to you by writing your negative thoughts in your journal.

The following quiz is another way for you to identify feelings and when you have them. Please put your answers in your journal so you can see how the changes you are making affect your life.

Feeling Identification

Answer the following questions as quickly and naturally as possible.

I limit my happiness by _____

I hate myself when _____

I hate myself for _____

I get mad at myself when _____

Right now, I feel guilty for _____

When I think of the future I feel _____

because _____

Sadness is _____

Miserable is _____

I worry too much about _____

Relief is _____

If I had my life to do over again, I would _____

I should stop worrying about _____

The Rebuttal Technique

In the rebuttal technique, you note your automatic negative thoughts and you analyze your thoughts in relationship to all of the ten distortions. If your automatic negative thought is any of the distortions, you need to change or refute it and make a rebuttal statement.

Example One

THOUGHT: "I can't do anything right."

COGNITIVE DISTORTIONS: All-or-none thinking. Mental filter. Emotional reasoning. Labeling and possibly blame.

REBUTTALS: "That's not true. I am good at a number of things." "I'm not perfect. No one is." "I'm too hard on myself. I'm good at..."

Example Two

THOUGHT: "It's hopeless; I'm bound to be depressed forever."

COGNITIVE DISTORTIONS: Mental filter. Jumping to conclusions (fortune-telling). Emotional reasoning. Labeling.

REBUTTALS: "If I follow the blueprint in this book, I can get better." "I'm depressed because the way I think is depressing." "Doing the exercises in this book will help me start to see the light at the end of the tunnel."

Example Three

THOUGHT: "Because of the seriousness of what I did, I deserve to feel guilty."

COGNITIVE DISTORTIONS: Mental filter. *Should* statement. Personalization and blame.

REBUTTALS: "It's water under the bridge. All I can do is try to learn from my mistake and not do it again." "Everyone deserves forgiveness." "I am trying to improve my life; I need to let go of the guilt."

Example Four

THOUGHT: "It's not safe to trust anyone. People are not trustworthy."

COGNITIVE DISTORTIONS: All-or-none thinking. Overgeneralization. Jumping to conclusions (mind-reading). Emotional reasoning.

REBUTTALS: "I possibly could be projecting onto others my feelings of distrust and unworthiness." "I need to give people a chance. I jump to conclusions too quickly."

Example Five

THOUGHT: "To be a worthwhile person, I must be successful at everything."

COGNITIVE DISTORTIONS: All-or-none thinking. Discounting the positive. Emotional reasoning. Labeling.

REBUTTALS: "Perfection is an illusion." "It's futile to try to reach for perfection; I'll instead just try to do my best." "I put too much pressure on myself; striving for perfection causes me to be anxious." "No one is perfect."

Example Six

THOUGHT: "It's not safe to let my guard down and be happy; something bad is bound to happen."

COGNITIVE DISTORTIONS: Overgeneralization. Mental filter. Jumping to conclusions (fortune-telling). Magnification. *Should* statement.

REBUTTALS: "I learned from this book to view stressors or events as challenges and not threats." "Ups and downs are part of everyday life." "I will take one day at a time and use the coping strategies I learned in this book."

Example Seven

THOUGHT: "I must worry about everything that could possibly happen to me from every angle or I won't be prepared to deal with it."

COGNITIVE DISTORTIONS: Mental filter. Jumping to conclusions (fortune-telling). Magnification. *Should* statements.

REBUTTALS: "What a waste of time, getting anxious over possible misfortunes." "I need to view catastrophes as possible, not probable." "No wonder I'm nervous, I'm focusing on the wrong things in life."

Using the Rebuttal Technique

Here's an ongoing practice to make good use of the rebuttal technique.

> Once you have uncovered your distorted thoughts, weighed them against the ten cognitive distortions, and formulated more positive affirmation statements (rebuttals), note the rebuttals on your phone or other electronic device (or on an index card). Keep them handy so you can use them as needed. You can also put them in your journal to keep track of your progress in dealing with distorted thoughts.

Years of living with negative thinking got you where you mentally are now. To recondition or retrain yourself to be in a better mental place will take some time, a conscious effort, and repeated practice. As one of my clients mentioned just yesterday, "It's a journey, but a journey that's worthwhile!"

You can compare your journey, your new learning experience, to learning how to drive or professionally type. When you initially learn to drive, it takes a lot

> *It takes hard practice before your conscious efforts become automatic.*

of conscious effort to stay focused on staying on the correct side of the road and in between the middle and side lines. When you first learn to type, it takes a focused, conscious effort to memorize the key locations and coordinate your key selection. It takes hard practice before your conscious efforts become automatic. The same is true in starting to use cognitive restructuring techniques such as reframing and the ten cognitive rebuttal techniques. Keep in mind that what you learn will be worth it in the end.

Remember, the Law of Resistance states that to become less depressed or less anxious, change the thought(s) that are causing the resistance and there is no more resistance. The Law of Association says like thoughts attract like thoughts. When you utilize such cognitive restructuring techniques as reframing, the ten cognitive distortion techniques, or *Boulders, Rocks, and Pebbles,* you are cognitively establishing rebuttals to stop faulty thinking in its tracks. If you get into the habit of using these time-tested techniques, you will start to feel successful and will become highly motivated to continue using them (Law of Motivation). You will then focus on good things and in turn will attract more good things into your life (Law of Attraction).

In Chapter 7 you will learn about the calming and therapeutic effects of mindfulness. You will be introduced to the mindfulness technique *Red Light/Green Light,* which will enable you to install cognitive rebuttals into your thinking. This technique will help you recondition or retrain yourself to take charge of your life.

SOLUTION SUMMARY

- There are clinically proven methods to empower change.

- Irrational thoughts equal mental disorders.
- Erickson's psychological stages help explain your current thinking.
- You can view your thinking as the captain of your ship.
- There are ten cognitive distortions.
- You can uncover your faulty thinking.
- Identifying feelings and rebuttals are valuable tools for changing faulty thinking.

7. Mindfulness is a Powerful Tool for Emotional Resetting

The ability to be present in the moment is a major component of mental wellness.

— *Dr. Abraham Maslow, psychologist*

In this chapter I will present some of the principles of mindfulness, or living in the moment, that I have found to be applicable to and effective in my model of therapy.

Benefits of Mindfulness

With practice, mindfulness can benefit you in many ways, including:

- Helping you more fully appreciate, participate in, and experience all the joy that life has to offer.
- Providing you with a much-needed space and time in which to purposefully act on, rather than impulsively react to, uncomfortable feelings, thus allowing you to activate your emotional reset button.
- Helping you detach yourself from needless worry and anxiety.
- Helping you consciously use cognitive restructuring techniques you have learned from this book — reframing, ten cognitive distortions, *Boulder, Rock, and Pebble*, and load shedding.

Mindfulness will help you to not only live in the moment but also embrace and absorb yourself in the splendor of life by savoring the moment. Following the mindfulness path leads to a way of living with joy, happiness, and tranquility.

One ultimate goal of mindfulness, living in the moment, is all about realizing and appreciating the beauty of living in every moment

> *Your life on this earth is not a dress rehearsal.*

of our lives, every day. More than just observing life, it requires our conscious, full attention and participation in life, moment by moment. Professionally, I encounter many people who observe life from the outside and do not participate in life to its fullest extent. Remember, your life on this earth is not a dress rehearsal.

Your Definition of Happiness?

It is no great secret that your definition of happiness will have a major impact on every aspect of your life — emotional, spiritual, financial, social, and physical.

> Take a moment and answer this question: What is your definition of happiness? Take your time and record your definition of happiness in your journal.

I often ask my clients this question and they respond with a wide range of answers, including more money, bigger house, expensive car, getting married, getting divorced, better job, etc. Some clients even comment, "I won't be happy until I get..." People who contend that happiness is something to be found outside of themselves turn happiness into an elusive pursuit that eventually leaves them feeling empty and unfulfilled. Their mantra is, "Things will be really great when..." Yet this feeling of greatness is temporary. How many times have you been excited to buy that big screen TV, new car, new video game, and then the excitement eventually fades?

> Some people chase happiness. Other people choose happiness. It depends on how much time you want to save.
>
> — *Anonymous*

You can *choose* to be happy. You can say *yes* to enjoying life. You can further embrace and enjoy life. Take notice of the world and start to enjoy living, moment by moment.

No matter what you are doing — exercising, cooking, driving to work, sitting on the porch — take notice of what surrounds you. For example, if you walk in the morning, really focus on the different trees, the buildings, animals, the sky, the sun, and try to use all your senses.

> Pick up an orange and hold it in your hand. Really start to notice it. Now, feel the orange in your hand. What does it feel like? Now, examine its color. What is the color? Now, put the orange in the other hand. Is it soft or hard? Squeeze it gently. What do you feel? Now, smell the orange. What do you smell? Now, peel the orange and notice the inner skin of the orange. What does it look like? What is the texture of the inner skin? What is its color? What does it smell like? Now, place a small slice of the orange in your mouth but don't eat it. Move the slice around in your mouth and notice every aspect of it. Notice its texture and taste. Now, bite the orange. Notice what it is like to put your teeth into it. Finish chewing and swallow it. Notice how that feels.

The purpose of this exercise is to enhance your awareness and ability to focus on the moment, the here and now. Focusing on your present experience also helps you to focus less on thoughts that could cause fears and anxieties about the future and guilt or regret about the past. When you are living in the moment, in essence you are saying, "These things that I usually take for granted, these wonders and small enjoyments in life, deserve my attention."

As I wrote this chapter, it was thundering and raining. I took the time to really hear, see, and feel the experience. I was truly becoming part of a greater universe — what Buddhist monks call "being one with everything." When you are mindful, you are more likely to experience yourself as part of the universe, as part of humanity, not just a bystander or victim.

In the future, no matter what is happening at the moment, no matter what you are doing — savor it. Use all your senses to enjoy that cup of coffee, prepare and eat breakfast, take a shower, look at God's creatures. These acts are the opposite of taking life for granted.

Some other things you may want to enjoy may be listening to a bird's song, watching a dog or cat sleep, watching the ripples on a pond or lake, really noticing the sunrise or sunset, noticing the shapes of trees and plants…this list can go on and on.

Stop Habituating

> Look at everything as though you were seeing it for the first or last time, then your time on earth will be filled with glory.
>
> — *Betty Smith*

Habituation is a psychological term that refers to the concept that we get used to things and tend to take things for granted. Habituation not only decreases happiness, it also drains away the joy and appreciation for many of the good things in our lives. Left unconfronted, habituation can suck the life from the experiences of our most treasured possessions: spouse, friends, children, work, and recreation.

To live in the present, you have to focus on what you are doing now and let go of every other thought. Your mind will keep on attempting to distract you, but continue to refocus yourself on your present activity.

If any thoughts that are not related to your present attention surface, discard them. Release them and continue doing what you are doing at the moment. When your mind wanders to the past or to the uncertainties of the future, refute and release those thoughts or simply ignore them.

Your mind has been trained or conditioned to reflect on the past and the future. You can retrain your mind, but it does take practice. Try to practice staying in the moment on a daily basis. You will then learn how not to take life for granted and will tend to embrace life on a daily basis.

So, stop habituating by not taking life for granted. By living in the moment, you will start to create a powerful and lasting foundation for a happy, peaceful life.

Mindfulness Decreases Rumination

Instead of getting stuck in your head and worrying, you
can let yourself go.
— *Dr. Steven Schueller, psychologist*

By utilizing mindfulness techniques, you can prevent yourself from
negative thinking about past failures, inadequacies, and guilt.
Mindfulness keeps you from reminiscing and ruminating about past
should haves and *could haves* that wear you down. It can also keep you
from ruminating about future uncertainties.

When you savor, and immerse yourself in, living in the moment and
using all your senses to enjoy drinking a cold beverage, eating a Danish
pastry, or enjoying a good book or the clouds — when you emerge into
and savor the present, you are redirecting your focus to the goodness
around you and diverting your attention from past guilts and future
concerns.

When you live in the moment, your problems disappear. There is no
stress at that moment, no guilt from the past at that moment, and nothing
to worry about in the future at that moment. You are focused on only
what is happening right now!

You can't change what happened in the past by rethinking it again
and again. And the present is not the time to ruminate about the future.

At this time, in the moment, the present is all you have that is
important. Living in the moment actually empowers you because you are
in control. Only you can control the moment. You have no control over
the past, and at that moment no particular concerns about the future.

If you have intrusive thoughts, release them from your mind or
ignore them and continue doing what you are doing at that moment.

For years your mind has been trained, conditioned to reflect on guilt
about the past or anxieties about the future. You can retrain your brain,
but it takes practice. Practice mindfulness, little by little, on a daily basis.
Start out utilizing mindfulness for small amounts of time and gradually
increase the time invested in mindfulness. You will learn to not take this
precious life for granted, and will tend to embrace and discover a new

life on a daily basis. You will find that you will become more patient and accepting of life's circumstances, as well as more emotionally stable when confronted with uncomfortable stressors, life events, and situations.

Mindfulness and Cognitive Restructuring

During my years as a therapist, I have found certain aspects of mindfulness to be applicable along with the cognitive restructuring techniques presented in this book. By practicing mindfulness, you can be more proficient in responding to old situations with a choice, rather than repeating old self-defeating patterns and habits. Mindfulness can help you access your thoughts and feelings without immediately placing judgment on them, so you don't get emotionally caught up in the guilt from the past and the uncertainty and anxieties of the future.

Mindfulness offers you the time necessary to recognize that you are in the midst of thinking uncomfortable, dysfunctional thoughts, so you don't have to get caught up in self-deprecating thought chatter. Mindfulness allows you to take note of your thoughts at a particular time without resorting to intense emotional overreaction.

Mindfulness can be a powerful tool for changing habitual emotional responses which sabotage your ability to think clearly, act responsibly, and live a meaningful, productive life. Make an attempt to apply mindfulness techniques daily and make them a part of your life. When you repeatedly practice the *Red Light/Green Light* technique described later in this chapter, you are actually reconditioning your thoughts by learning to stop faulty thinking, just as you learned or became conditioned to stop at a red light while driving.

Every time you encounter an angry or negative emotion that threatens to dominate you, such as irritation, fear, anxiety, despair, guilt, or sadness, practice mindfulness.

Mindfulness and Social Anxiety

The act of being mindful and living in the moment can play an integral part in reducing social anxiety. Mindfulness blurs the lines between yourself and other people. When you are mindful, you are more likely to experience yourself as more connected to the group and part of humanity. You gain a feeling of being one with the universe.[20] Conversely, when you focus on yourself, you create a self-defeating pattern of negative self-talk and chatter that further perpetuates social pressure and social anxieties. By utilizing mindfulness, by concentrating on what is going on in the room and not on yourself, you naturally become less self-conscious and more able and willing to become part of the group. You feel more comfortable and willing to participate rather than being an outside observer.

Some helpful techniques to encourage you to become more immersed in the group and to become more a part of the group are

- Ask someone in the group an interesting question.
- Ask a member for advice and really listen to the response.
- Address each member by the first name.
- Don't criticize or condemn anyone's suggestions.
- Offer praise to someone who deserves it.
- Really pay attention when others speak and, if need be, ask for clarification of their comments.
- Speak to each member as if you really care and pay attention to others' observations.
- Most importantly, listen, listen, listen!

By redirecting your full attention to the group or to an acquaintance, you minimize focusing on yourself and your self-worth.[21] Keep in mind that no matter whether things are great or small, you are part of a singular moment where all things come together. You are part of a greater universe.[22]

> Life is a journey, not a destination.
> — *Ralph Waldo Emerson*

Mindfulness can help you shift your focus, not only to accomplish long-term goals but also to learn to appreciate and enjoy the day-to-day journey.

Kelly's Struggle to Succeed

As a child and later as an adult, Kelly was focused on proving herself. At 33 years of age, she was driven, if not obsessed, with the need to be successful. Granted, she eventually accomplished some of her goals, but at a price. She initiated counseling, as so many do, because she was miserable. Laden with stress and anxiety, her life held little joy and no sense of accomplishment. Every day she was frustrated and anxious because she could never accomplish her high daily goals. Every day, because she did not meet all of her goals, she would emotionally beat herself up.

Here's a snapshot of her thoughts: "You're fine until you make a mistake." "If I'm not working, I'm not productive." "Everything has to be done today." "I never get done what I want to get done; I could always be doing more." and "If I don't adhere to my exact planned schedule, then the day is a waste."

Socially, she felt that everyone had to live up to her expectations and that other people should perform at her level.

Kelly's dysfunctional thinking process made it virtually impossible for her to ever achieve her goals, let alone enjoy the journey. Kelly was a prisoner of her dysfunctional way of thinking. She was well on her way to a life of panic attacks, unhappiness, and misery. Isn't it ironic? What she thought was so important to achieve happiness and contentment caused her so much emotional unrest and pain. She needed to learn to not only modify her goals, but to enjoy the daily journey as she worked to meet her goals. Kelly also needed to find the path to a more peaceful, content existence by living in the moment.

Mindfulness Techniques

Breathing

Mindfulness is a powerful resource for changing habitual emotional reactions and automatic behaviors. One way to do this is by utilizing your ability to breathe.

An effective way to reground yourself to the present is to focus on your breathing. When you take a conscious, purposeful breath of air, you are redirecting and anchoring your awareness to the present, to this moment. There is magic in a breath. When you take a deliberate breath, it actually improves your serotonin level, which produces calmness.

Breath is available to us throughout our lives and can conveniently serve to condition or reground us to stop and take time to refocus on the present. With a small amount of practice, my clients associate taking a deliberate breath with a feeling of well-being and calmness. They often mention that taking a deliberate breath while thinking the word *relax* or *calm* allows them to let go of negative feelings.

As you will soon discover, the seemingly simple act of taking a breath will allow you the necessary time and calmness to redirect old self-defeating, self-deprecating messages that have left you with feelings of despair, disappointment, depression, and anxiety. In essence, a breath affords you the time to redirect your thinking and to make better choices about activating your emotional-reset button.

Red Light/Green Light Technique[23]

The *Red Light/Green Light* technique is a way to recondition your thoughts by learning to stop faulty thinking, just as you learned or became conditioned to stop at a red light while driving. This mindfulness technique increases your self-control and truly activates your emotional-reset button. Additionally, you are conditioning yourself to think good thoughts, which will naturally attract more good thoughts and good things to you.

Red Light Mode

When you feel uncomfortable, angry, or other negative emotions, you enter the red light mode — you stop reasoning. In this mode, the frontal lobe of the brain turns off. The frontal lobe is the smart part of your brain, the problem-solving, executive, reasoning area. When the frontal lobe is turned off, the limbic system takes over — and you do stupid stuff! You emotionally react or act out.

STOP!

Breathe deeply, inhaling for four seconds and exhaling for eight seconds. Let yourself become calm.

Yellow Light Mode

Appraise the situation.

THINK!

- What is my old pattern here?
- What resources or options do I have right here in the present moment?
- How can I reframe a *threat* to a *challenge*?
- Do I need to load-shed?
- How can I utilize the ten cognitive distortion techniques?
- How can I utilize *Boulder, Stone, and Pebble*?
- Is my concern possible or probable?
- Is this something in my control? If not, do I need to let go of it?

Green Light Mode

When you find the answer, you reactivate your common sense, the reasoning part of your brain — the frontal lobe:

GO!

You feel more comfortable, peaceful and are able to purposefully act, not just react. Congratulate yourself on a job well done!

Autogenic Meditation

There are many forms of meditation, so many in fact that it is not possible for me to summarize them all in this book. Of these, I have found that autogenic meditation is easy to practice, can be an integral tool for positive change and growth, and can help you recover from anxiety, stress, and tension. Persons who practice autogenic meditation twice a day fall asleep more easily and sleep more deeply. They think more clearly and are less prone to anxiety or depression. People who meditate for 15-20 minutes, once or twice a day, age more slowly and are less likely to become ill.

Repeat the phrases in the following sets silently, in your mind, three times. Say the phase in a quiet, thoughtful way. Pause after each set and notice how you feel. Focus on your feelings for two or three breaths. Practice each set of exercises until you are quite comfortable with them.[24]

Set One

- I feel quiet.
- I relax easily.
- My right arm feels heavy and relaxed.
- My left arm feels heavy and relaxed.
- My arms feel heavy and relaxed.
- My right leg feels heavy and relaxed.
- My left leg feel heavy and relaxed.
- My arms and legs feel heavy and relaxed.
- My hips and stomach are quiet and relaxed.
- My shoulders are heavy and relaxed.
- My breathing is calm and regular.
- My face is smooth and quiet.
- I am beginning to feel quite relaxed.

Set Two

- My right hand is warm.
- My left hand is warm.
- Warmth flows into my hands.
- My hands are warm.
- My right foot is warm.
- My left foot is warm.
- My hands and feet are warm.
- Warmth flows into my hands and feet.
- My eyes are comfortably warm and peaceful.

- My forehead is cool and my eyes are warm.
- I am warm and peaceful.

Set Three

- I am beginning to feel quite relaxed.
- I am learning to feel calm and confident.
- I talk about what I appreciate and I feel confident.
- I appreciate others and myself.
- My life has many blessings I overlook.
- I am beginning to see my own blessings.
- I appreciate my life more and more.

Set Four

- My breathing is calm and regular.
- My heartbeat is calm and regular.
- I am at peace.
- Sounds and sights around me contribute to peace.
- Peace goes with me throughout my day.
- There is nothing to bother me and nothing to disturb me.

Set Five

- I am not required to think now.
- I don't have to think now.
- Thoughts are not important now.
- There is nothing to bother or disturb me now.
- I am not interested in thinking now.
- There is nothing to bother me and nothing to disturb me.

By means of meditation, in addition to becoming more aware of your feelings and thoughts, you can practice and rehearse new, healthier thinking patterns. While in the relaxed state, you can further determine where you would like to be and how it differs from where you are now.

Autogenic meditation can help you control your emotional state and activate your emotional reset button. If you want to practice and rehearse associating new, healthier thought patterns with old reactions, use Sets One through Four and eliminate Set Five.

As you visualize and rehearse, you can use *Red Light/Green Light* to deal with uncomfortable feelings and the need to replace old, dysfunctional, refuted thought patterns with new healthy thoughts.

Remarkable Scientific Findings about Meditation

- Harvard Medical School professor Dr. Herbert Benson found that people who meditate countered the stress-induced fight-or-flight response and achieved a calmer, happier state of mind.[25]
- University of Massachusetts professor Dr. Jon Kabat-Zinn helped more than 14,000 people manage their pain by teaching them the meditation technique of focusing on what their pain feels like and accepting it, rather than fighting it.[26]
- Meditation has been proven to slow aging, relieve irritable bowel syndrome, improve the symptoms of psoriasis, and boost the immune response.[27]
- Studies published in the *Journal of Neuroscience* in 2013 showed that meditation assists people to stop smoking, overcome anxiety, and lose weight.[28]
- Recent studies found that eight weeks of daily meditations have a calming effect on the brain's amygdala which reduces fear.[29]
- A 2013 study published in *Psychological Science* suggested that meditation involving thoughts of loving and kindness produces more positive emotions. Meditating individuals are better able to calm themselves when they have negative feelings.[30]
- That 2013 study also reported that meditation reduces heart rate and blood pressure.[31]
- Meditation increases the electrical energy in the happiness center of the brain.[32]

At this stage in your journey, you are probably aware of the majority of your specific faulty thought(s). The thought(s) may include "I can't do anything right." "I have to be perfect or I failed." "It's not safe to be happy, or something bad will happen." "Because of my past sins, I must punish myself." "Everybody should live up to my expectations." "I feel like a loser so I must be one." "The world should be as I expect it to be." "No one likes me." "I'll always be depressed." "I'll always be anxious." etc.

Remember, your feelings are a direct reflection of what you are thinking. So when you feel uncomfortable, note the thought and practice utilizing *Red Light/Green Light*: stop, breathe deeply, appraise the situation, and make rebuttals.

If you would like to pursue a more in-depth study of mindfulness, I suggest you read *Cultivating Lasting Happiness: A 7-Step Guide to Mindfulness*, by Terry Fralich, LCPC, JD.

In the following chapters I outline how mindfulness and the *Red Light/Green Light* technique can help you better handle real-life problems and scenarios such as marriage, children, toxic relationships, anxiety, and depression.

SOLUTION SUMMARY

- Mindfulness is a powerful emotional reset tool.
- Mindfulness benefits include living in the moment and detaching from needless worry and anxiety.
- You can choose to be happy.
- Habituating and ruminating make your life worse.
- The power of the breath is magical.
- The mindfulness techniques of breathing, *Red Light/Green Light,* and autogenic meditation promote cognitive restructuring and reduce social anxiety.
- The benefits of meditation have been proven scientifically.

Section II.
The Blueprint for Change and Happiness

8. Taking Charge of Your Anxiety

The belief that one's reality is the only reality is the most dangerous of all delusions.

— Paul Watzawick,
psychologist, philosopher, and author

Anxiety, stress, and fear do not exist independently of you in the world. They simply do not exist, even though we talk about them as if they do. When it comes to anxiety, and especially panic attacks, many people feel that they can never have control over these extremely disturbing emotional reactions. They become delusional about their anxiety — they develop the false belief that what is happening is something outside themselves and the only solution is a magic pill. They feel it is what it is and rush to relieve their symptoms and solve the problem with a pill. Fortunately, for most people both anxiety and panic attacks are easily treated by therapy, because these emotional responses are not a result of actual danger.

Distinction between Stress, Anxiety, and Phobias

Generally speaking, stress is a reaction to a specific stressor such as financial problems, taking an interview, or giving a speech. Typically, when the stressor goes away, so does the stress.

Anxiety is an emotional state due to uncertainty about the future. Anxiety is a state of intense worry, even when there is no apparent reason for it. It's a general sense that something bad is going to happen. As you will discover in this chapter, people with anxiety disorders are troubled by the *what ifs*.

Phobias are specific irrational fears. There are numerous phobias, including fear of spiders, fear of crossing bridges, fear of driving in traffic, fear of flying, and fear of the dark, to name a few.

This chapter focuses on anxiety and panic attacks due to anxiety. A few of the symptoms of anxiety are racing heart, rapid breathing or hyperventilation, chest pains, nausea, sweating, dizziness, tingling, and numbness. It's no wonder that many of my anxious clients exclaim that they are going crazy, losing their mind, or having a nervous breakdown. Refer to Appendix E for a more complete list of possible physical and psychological symptoms of anxiety and panic.

What is Generalized Anxiety Disorder?

The symptoms of Generalized Anxiety Disorder (GAD) include constant worrying about small or large concerns, restlessness and feeling constantly on edge, fatigue, difficulty concentrating, irritability, muscle tension or aches, being easily startled, insomnia, sweating, nausea or diarrhea, and shortness of breath.

People who have GAD are consumed with excessive worry for no apparent reason. For example, people with GAD may be concerned about their safety or the safety of their children. Frequently, they have feelings of impending doom, that something bad is about to happen. They are constantly replaying their *what ifs*.

What Really Happens When You Suffer from a So-called Nervous Breakdown

Anxiety, it just stops your life.

– *Amanda Seyfried, actress*

When we are faced with the possibility of actual danger, such as a car accident, a robbery, a vicious dog attack, a tornado, or an earthquake, our sympathetic nervous system, which is part of the autonomic nervous system, prepares for fight or flight. Survival emotions go on full alert. We then become anxious, fearful, panicky, startled, and hypervigilant to the situation. The sympathetic nervous system is an adaptive mechanism which stops digestion and redirects blood from the stomach to our muscles, increases heart rate, increases sweating, and causes dry mouth and tremors. Our bodies go on full alert and get ready to fight or flee to survive.

When you suffer a so-called nervous breakdown, your nerves don't break down. You are responding irrationally to perceived threats or danger. Anxiety is enhanced by catastrophizing — focusing on the worst possible scenarios. You feel vulnerable and in danger. You feel you have no control over your anxiety and you feel unsafe. Due to the *perceived* threat, your thinking becomes cloudy. You lose proper perspective on your life and on reality, and lose confidence in your ability to deal with life.

When you experience an anxiety or panic attack, or even fear you are having one, every system in your body is affected, including:

- Physiological: "I'm sweating." "My heart is racing." "I'm breathing way too fast."
- Cognitive: "I can't think."
- Emotional: "I feel terrified." "I'm a hopeless case."
- Behavioral: "I can't stop pacing." "My speech is slurred."
- Motivational: "I need to flee this situation." "I have to avoid…"

How Anxiety Attacks Sustain Themselves

If the mind causes anxiety and panic attacks, the mind can take it away.

– *Dr. William Matta*

Panic attacks due to anxiety are perpetuated in two ways: by dysfunctional thoughts and by physical feedback.

People who suffer from anxiety and anxiety-produced panic attacks become psychologically ready to react to every false alarm. They become proficient at being ready for "red alert" even when they are not in danger. Their ability to reason becomes impaired, and their thinking becomes illogical. Anxiety creates a vicious cycle. For example, your heart beats faster, you start sweating, and your "red alert" thoughts surface. The more you become aware of being anxious, the faster your heart beats, the more threatened you feel, and the cycle escalates.

When I first inform my clients that it is your mind or, more precisely, your thoughts that cause anxiety attacks and, therefore, your mind can take the anxiety away, some become enlightened while others think it's nonsense. Again, the major culprit for emotional problems is our thoughts. When we are anxious, our thoughts activate the fight-or-flight response. Conversely, our minds can deactivate or de-energize the emergency fight-or-flight response, especially when the threat is not real.

You may retort, as many of my clients have, "But my panic attacks are real. I physically experience them. My heart pounds, I hyperventilate, I feel dizzy, and I'm shaky." I inform my clients that, yes, the physical symptoms are real, but they are activated by how you perceive the situation and by thinking that you are in imminent danger. Thus, your anxiety and panic attacks are sustained by your thoughts, and as you will soon learn — by the *what ifs*.

> In addition to our thoughts, and the *what ifs*, one's
> visceral or bodily sensations serve to perpetuate the
> problem.
>
> — *Dr. William Matta*

One of the most difficult tasks or fears for many people, even worse than death, is the thought of giving a speech. A scenario that often develops is the speaker, being anxious, is on guard and thus readily perceives cues from the audience that feed the nervousness. The speaker also becomes aware of any internal nervous cues, such as memory loss, sweating, shaking, or stuttering and — guess what? These physical sensations make matters worse. Consequently the forgetting or sweating or stuttering or shaking gets worse, the *uh ohs* take over, and the cycle feeds on itself. What you want to avoid —flight — is what your body and mind do!

Stopping the Emergency Fight-or-Flight Response

He who fears something gives it power over him.
— *Moorish proverb*

The fight-or-flight response can produce some scary physical symptoms. The first time or two a symptom happens to you, it is worthwhile to get it checked out. That's taking care of the *uh ohs*. When the symptoms are known to be part of a fight-or-flight response, you can use the ideas in this book to handle them. To put your mind at ease, here are some facts that will help you deal with the fight-or-flight response from *The Anxiety & Phobia Workbook* by Edmund J. Bourne.[33]

Fact 1: A panic attack is not a heart attack.

A racing heart and palpitations are frightening but, if they are caused by an anxiety attack, they are not dangerous. A healthy heart can beat 200 beats per minute, or more, for days and weeks. Some anxious people even report chest pains in the upper left portion of the chest. During a true heart attack, the most common symptom is continuous pain and pressure or a crushing sensation in the center of your chest. That pain is intensified with physical activity and tends to diminish with rest. When you feel the panic attack start, say to yourself, "It's only anxiety. I'll relax myself — it will go away." Remember, good thoughts attract more good thoughts.

Fact 2: An anxiety attack cannot cause you to suffocate.

During an anxiety attack your breathing may become restricted and you can't catch your breath. You feel like you will suffocate. What is really happening is that your neck and chest muscles are tightening, which reduces your respiration capability. I tell clients that when this happens, breathing into a paper bag will alleviate the feeling. Use self-talk: "I can deal with this. I can relax. I'll blow into a paper bag or my hand until it ceases."

Fact 3: An anxiety attack cannot cause you to faint.

When you experience a panic attack, you may feel lightheaded, which can evoke the *uh oh* of "I'm going to faint." The lightheadedness is caused by the blood circulation to your brain being slightly reduced because your breathing is more rapid. This is not dangerous and can be relieved by slowly breathing from your belly through your nose and then, if possible, taking a walk, breathing naturally, and letting the lightheadedness gradually subside. Remember the Law of Association: like thoughts attract more like thoughts. Tell yourself: "Relax, I'll breathe from my belly through my nose. I'll be okay. It's only my body reacting."

Fact 4: A panic attack cannot cause you to lose your balance.

Frequently anxiety causes dizziness. More than likely tension is affecting the semicircular canals in your inner ear, which regulates your balance, thus you feel dizzy or that things are spinning. Invariably this sensation will dissipate and is not dangerous. If these sensations last longer than a few seconds, you may want to consult your physician to check for infection, allergies, or inner ear problems. If you really do lose your balance, it may be something more serious and you should seek immediate medical attention. Self talk: "So what? I have been here before. I'll take a deep breath, calm down, and it will pass."

Fact 5: If you get wobbly knees, you will not fall or stop walking.

Adrenaline is secreted during an anxiety attack, which dilates the blood vessels in your legs, thus causing blood to accumulate in your legs and not fully circulate. This produces a sensation of weakness, or "jelly legs." This reaction is just a sensation and your legs are strong. They won't give way. Just allow this reaction to pass. Tell yourself, "My mind caused this, my mind can take it away. I need to breathe normally and calm down."

Fact 6: A panic attack cannot cause you to lose control of yourself or go crazy.

As a result of all the physical reactions that can possibly occur during an anxiety attack, my clients often say that they are "losing control" or "going crazy." Keep in mind that this is your body reacting to your thoughts' *what ifs* and *uh ohs*. Actually, these sensations are simply due to stress hormones which slightly shift the balance of blood circulation in your brain. No one goes crazy in a sudden, spontaneous way. Severe mental disorders take years to develop. Loss of control during anxiety attacks is simply a myth. Self-talk: "Accept the feeling. It cannot hurt me. Breathe, be calm, distract myself. It's only anxiety. I'll emotionally reset myself."

Facts about Medication

Although medications can be helpful, they shouldn't be thought of as cures. Anxiety medication can provide temporary relief but it doesn't treat the underlying causes of anxiety. Once you stop taking the medication, the symptoms of anxiety often return in full force. So, while drug treatment can be beneficial, it is by no means enough.

Anti-anxiety drugs such as benzodiazepines (Xanax, Valium, Ativan, and Klonopin) relieve anxiety by slowing down the central nervous system. They can work quickly and they alleviate panic attacks, but they often have side effects, and the higher the dose, the more pronounced the side effects. Common side effects include drowsiness, depression, dizziness, impaired thinking, forgetfulness, blurred vision, confusion, nausea, and slurred speech. And some people react to these medications with just the opposite of the intended purpose: mania, rage, hostility, and even hallucinations.

You should also be aware that such medications are also habit-forming and physically addictive. These consequences are often difficult to stop once started. One of my friends stopped taking Xanax and was still experiencing hallucinations a year later. As we were walking one day, he told me that trees and other objects were jumping out at him.

Other medications that were originally approved for the treatment of depression have been found to relieve the symptoms of anxiety. These are the selective serotonin reuptake inhibiting (SSRI) antidepressants (Prozac, Zoloft, Paxil, Lexapro, Celexa, Cymbalta, and Effexor). They function by regulating the serotonin levels in the brain to elevate mood and calm anxiety. Antidepressants are often preferred to benzodiazepines because they are not addictive. However, antidepressants take at least four to six weeks to begin to provide relief and are not effective on an as-needed basis. Although physical addiction is not an issue with antidepressants, a form of rebound withdrawal can occur with these antidepressants if even one dose is missed. This can result in extreme depression, anxiety, irritability, fatigue, flu-like symptoms, and insomnia. Never stop taking or reduce any medication without permission from your prescriber.

Buspar (buspirone) is an anti-anxiety drug that functions as a mild tranquilizer. It relieves anxiety by increasing serotonin in the brain, like the SSRIs do. It takes at least one to two months to start working on anxiety. It is not addictive and withdrawal effects are minimal. Because the risk of dependence is minimal and it has no serious drug interactions, it is a good option for older people and people with a history of substance abuse. However, the downside is that it takes a long time to begin to provide relief and thus cannot be used on an as-needed basis.

Medications may treat some symptoms of anxiety but, no matter what, they can't change the underlying causes of anxiety or provide you with a plan or method to deal with the anxiety.

Research has shown that the most effective treatment for anxiety is cognitive-behavioral techniques, many of which I have outlined in this book.

Alex's Perpetual Cycle of Anxiety and Panic

Alex was a 34-year-old engineer who worked at a major company for about two years. He entered counseling because he was close to being fired due to his excessive absences from work. Alex had been married for eight years and had two children, Lori, age three, and Bryan, age eight. Alex suffered from Generalized Anxiety Disorder — he worried almost obsessively about his children being harmed or kidnapped. Lori was in a good preschool and Bryan was in a suburban elementary school. In reality, both children were safe and happy in their schools. Nevertheless, in his thoughts, Alex was sure something bad was going to happen to them. And his gut reactions, his bodily reactions, proved to him that his anxiety was real and warranted.

Specifically, when Alex ruminated on potential harm that could happen to his children, he became nauseated and started to tremble and sweat. He then focused on these physical sensations. Consequently these sensations intensified, his emergency response system activated, and he went on red alert. The act of going on red alert only served to further perpetuate an anxiety attack, thus reinforcing the delusion that something bad was going to happen to his children. During this process, he developed what I call a case of the *what ifs,* as well as the *uh ohs*. In his case, the *what ifs* were "What if Lori or Bryan are kidnapped?" and the *uh ohs* were "My gut feeling is one of nervousness. Uh oh, it must be true. They are in danger!"

The major point is that physical uneasiness, along with his *what ifs* and *uh ohs*, enhanced his anxiety state, making him think something bad was about to happen to his children.

The primary goal of my treatment with Alex was to stop him from focusing on the *what ifs* and *uh ohs*. When you use the principles and

> *Your mind causes it, and your mind can take it away.*

laws discussed in this book, you deactivate your red alert system and activate your emotional reset button, and then there is no more emergency. Remember, your mind causes it, and your mind can take it away.

A primary goal in treating anxiety is to help the client replace saying "what if?" with "so what!" When you can say "so what," you are literally activating the parasympathetic part of the autonomic nervous system which reverses the fight-or-flight emergency system. At the end of Part I we discussed ways to return your body to a calm, manageable state.

During his counseling sessions, I learned that Alex's father was an alcoholic. When his father got drunk, his behavior became erratic and he got angry and lashed out at Alex for no apparent reason. Alex had a younger sister, but the father took his frustrations out mainly on Alex. His father blacked out and didn't remember the incident. The next morning, after the damage was done, his father, not remembering what happened, was pleasant to Alex. This further confused and troubled Alex. After such an alcoholic episode, Alex asked himself "Why would my father act so mean to me at night and be so caring in the morning?" "What am I doing wrong?" "What do I need to do to win my father's approval?" "When is it going to happen again?" "How can I prevent my dad from getting so angry?"

Alex became hypervigilant, looking for any potentially dangerous or threatening scenario that could provoke his father to fury. Eventually Alex developed a sense of helplessness because no matter what he did, no matter how hypervigilant he became, it didn't matter, because when his father drank, he often displaced his anger onto Alex.

As is the case with many adult children of alcoholics, because Alex's childhood was so erratic and chaotic, as an adult he needed to be in control. He attempted to maintain control of his feelings and behavior at all costs. His need to be in control was a reaction to his intense fear — fear that his life would get worse and possibly spiral out of control, as it did growing up in his household. Whenever he felt that he could not control situations, feelings, or behavior, he became extremely anxious.

Over the years, as a survival technique Alex developed an emotional state of constant uneasiness and general tension — anxiety — while waiting for the other shoe to drop. He became hypervigilant and would catastrophize that something bad was about to happen. His futile attempts to control things that were out of his control only perpetuated his worry, anxiety, and feelings of helplessness and hopelessness. In addition to being anxious, he became depressed. His anxiety and fear of the uncertainties of the future permeated every aspect of his life including his marriage, career, and feelings about himself. He became especially anxious about his beloved daughter Lori and he focused many of his *what ifs* on her.

In his heart he knew something bad would happen to Lori. Alex believed that if he didn't worry about all of the possible scenarios, he would lose control of the situation, and the thing he didn't worry about would happen. Without therapy Alex was doomed to a life of needless worry, anxiety, and despair. Even more concerning was the fact that he was starting to resort to taking the deadly combination of alcohol and tranquilizers to escape from and soothe his troubled emotional state. During the initial stages of counseling, he was not yet consciously aware that he was on the way to the destructive substance use cycle that he detested in his father's behavior.

Obviously, Alex's complex and severe problems could not be resolved overnight —in addition to cognitive restructuring, his treatment plan included psychotherapy and AA meetings. That said, a major part of his therapy revolved around cognitive restructuring, which gave him insight into his faulty assumptions and the negative thinking that fueled his anxiety. He came to realize how his irrational *what ifs* were perpetually activating his emergency fight-or-flight system, specifically his fear that something bad was about to happen, especially to his daughter. He also gained insight into how, through the Law of Resistance, his negative thoughts kept him from becoming less anxious, and how, though the Law of Association, his habitual anxious thoughts escalated his unfounded concern that something bad was going to happen.

He also became proficient at letting go of things that were out of his control, using the liberating concept of probable versus possible. Lastly, he developed the habit of reframing the uncertainties of the future so what he used to perceive as potential threats were now thought of as future adventures and opportunities to enhance, enjoy, and savor life.

Alex's Dysfunctional Thinking Process

Here are the pivotal self-defeating thoughts that created Alex's resistance to better managing his anxiety. For your convenience, the ten cognitive distortions are listed in Appendix D.

THOUGHT: "I must stay alert or something bad will happen."

COGNITIVE DISTORTIONS: All-or-none thinking; mental filter; jumping to conclusions (fortune-telling); magnification

THOUGHT: "If I don't worry about possible misfortunes, they will happen."
COGNITIVE DISTORTIONS: All-or-none thinking; overgeneralization; jumping to conclusions (fortune-telling); magnification

THOUGHT: "I need to be in full control of my world or my life will fall apart."
COGNITIVE DISTORTIONS: All-or-none thinking; jumping to conclusions (fortune-telling); magnification

THOUGHT: "The world is evil. I need to protect and prevent all bad things from happening to my family."
COGNITIVE DISTORTIONS: All-or-none thinking; overgeneralization; jumping to conclusions (fortune-telling); magnification

THOUGHT: "My body doesn't lie. When I get a nervous stomach, something bad is about to happen."
COGNITIVE DISTORTIONS: All-or-none thinking; emotional reasoning

THOUGHT: "It's hopeless. I'm bound to feel anxious forever. I've always been this way."
COGNITIVE DISTORTIONS: All-or-none thinking; mental filter; jumping to conclusions (fortune-telling); emotional reasoning; labeling

Alex's Affirmations for Letting Go of Control

> When we are no longer able to change a situation, we are challenged to change ourselves.
>
> — *Viktor Frankl*

During therapy, I provided Alex with these affirmations about letting go of things you can't control:

- To let go does not mean to stop caring; it means I can't do it for someone else.
- To let go is not to cut myself off, it's the realization that I can't control another.
- To let go is not to enable, but to allow learning from natural consequences.
- To let go is to admit powerlessness that means the outcome is not in my hands.
- To let go is not to try to change or blame another; it's to make the most of myself.
- To let go is not to care for, but to care about.
- To let go is not to fix, but to be supportive.
- To let go is not to judge, but to allow another to be a human being.
- To let go is not to be in the middle arranging all the outcomes, but to allow others to be in charge of their destinies.
- To let go is not to be overprotective; it's to permit another to face reality.
- To let go is not to deny, but to accept.
- To let go is not to nag, scold, or argue, but instead to search out my own shortcomings and correct them.
- To let go is not to adjust everything to my desires, but to take each day as it comes and cherish myself in it.
- To let go is not to criticize and regulate anybody, but to try to become what I dream I can be.
- To let go is not to regret the past, but to grow and live for the future.
- To let go is to fear less and love more.

Alex's Empowered Thinking Process

By using reframing, cognitive rebuttals, letting-go affirmations, and *Boulder, Rock, and Pebble*, Alex was able to transform his anxiety-provoking self-talk:

FROM: "I must stay alert or something bad will happen."

TO: "This constant state of tension is killing me. Even when I am on red alert, stuff happens. Life is full of its ups and downs. That's how we grow and develop."

FROM: "If I don't worry about possible misfortunes, they will happen."

TO: "My constant worrying about things isn't working. All I am doing is making myself anxious. Things happen if I worry or don't worry. I can't be in school, always protecting my children. I'm wearing myself out, trying to control things that are out of my control. I need to let go."

FROM: "I need to be in full control of my world or my life will fall apart."

TO: "No wonder I'm suffering from anxiety with that kind of thinking. No wonder I'm running around in circles. When I feel this way, I need to make rebuttals and to realize the difference between things or events that I can control, things I cannot control, and the things or events I can influence."

FROM: "The world is evil; I need to protect and prevent all bad things from happening to my family."

TO: "The world just is. There is some good as well as not so good in it. I need to let go of things that I cannot control and life at times will run its own course. We learn from adversity. Also, is it possible for me to experience a horrific event? Yes. Is it probable? No."

FROM: "My body doesn't lie, when I get a nervous stomach, something bad is about to happen."

TO: "That's only my body reacting to my anxious way of thinking. I can control this visceral sensation by distracting myself and making rebuttals. I can also use my autogenic training to arrest these sensations. So what? This will soon pass."

FROM: "It's hopeless; I'm bound to feel anxious forever. I've always been this way."

TO: "I now know how and why I've always been so anxious. Knowledge is power. I now have more control over my mental state than I thought I ever could. My thoughts have caused my anxiety; my thoughts can take it away. What a relief, I know I can reset my emotional state. What a sense of empowerment!"

What is ironic is that Alex gained control of his emotional life by relinquishing control. He learned how self-defeating and anxiety provoking it was to attempt to influence or control people and events that were out of his control. He was no longer a prisoner of his anxiety-evoking way of thinking.

By using the laws and principles outlined in this book, Alex became proficient at changing the *what ifs* to "so what." He consciously converted stressors from threats to challenges. He was able to change the thoughts that caused his resistance to becoming less anxious, and he was able to stop the self-defeating attraction of more anxiety-producing thoughts by pausing and then using the *Red Light/Green Light* technique, and making rebuttals. He rewired his brain and established anti-anxiety circuits. He learned how to activate his emotional-reset button, and his good thoughts begot more good thoughts, which in turn attracted good things to his life. He became more able to savor the moment. He projected confidence to others. He began to focus on what he wanted and not on what he feared. And at least once a day he utilized autogenic meditation to consciously reinforce his newly acquired behavior patterns. Alex learned to live life anew!

Resolving Your Anxiety

We have to learn to be our own best friends, because we fall too easily into the trap of being our own worst enemies.

– Robert Thorp

Due to the inherent limitations of a book, I may not have discussed the core beliefs of your anxiety. Nevertheless, you now have the tools to take the first step in taking your anxiety management into your awareness. When you feel anxious, do two things: Ask yourself the following probing questions to appraise your anxiety. Then design a plan for approaching what you fear.

Questions that will help you appraise your anxiety

- What are the circumstances that are causing me to feel anxious?
- What are my automatic thoughts?
- How am I making myself anxious?

Questions that will help you create a blueprint of responses to your fears

- What are the thoughts that are causing me to resist becoming less anxious?
- What are the specific anxious thoughts (Law of Association) that are causing me to feel anxious and/or to have a panic attack?
- What laws, principles, and techniques that I learned from this book can I apply to attack this problem?
- Remembering the grasshopper in the jar, do I believe I can change by taking it step by step?
- Knowing that the only place to break my stress or anxiety cycle is in my thoughts, what have I learned to do about it?
- How can I convert my stressor(s) from threats to challenges?
- How can I reframe the situation?
- Do I need to load-shed now?
- How can I use the ten cognitive distortions to refute my negative thoughts?
- How I can use *Boulders, Rocks, and Pebbles* to help with my problem?
- Is the anxiety-evoking situation possible or probable?
- What rebuttals have I established?
- What else do I have to do before I use *Red Light/Green Light?*
- How can I use autogenic meditation to help me accomplish my goal?
- Though I am working on this problem, how can I take time to savor the moment and enjoy my life right now?

- What affirmations can I use to maintain my positive thinking and confidence as I solve this problem and implement my plans?

More Suggested Affirmations

If you experience difficulty thinking of affirmations, the following affirmations may help you:

To prepare for an anxiety-producing situation, say:

- "I'll be okay. This is no big deal."
- "Once I get started, I'll be fine."
- "It's okay for me to feel nervous."
- "It's only anxiety, it will not kill me."

To confront and handle a situation, say:

- "I'll focus on what I want."
- "This doesn't have to be perfect. Perfection is an illusion."
- "I'll take one step at a time. I'll be okay."
- "I will think positive thoughts."

To cope with feeling overwhelmed, say:

- "I'll use distraction. It's only anxiety."
- "I'll take a deep breath and move on."
- "I can't let these feelings stop me. I need to move forward."

To reinforce success in handling anxiety, say:

- "I handled it. I'm proud of myself."
- "Congratulations, I did a really good job."
- "That was easier than I thought."

SOLUTION SUMMARY

- You can take charge of your anxiety.
- Anxiety attacks can't sustain themselves if you stop them.
- Six facts may help you stop the emergency fight-or-flight response.

- Medication for anxiety doesn't really solve the problem.
- Affirmations help you let go of control.
- You may be making yourself anxious and there are things you can do about it.

9. Taking Charge of Your Depression and Guilt

No one or no thing can depress you unless you allow it.
— *Viktor Frankl*

Over my many years of practicing psychotherapy, one of the most frequent disorders that I have successfully treated is depression. I have professionally encountered clients from ages 12 to 80 who were moderately to severely depressed. When depressed people enter counseling, most express feeling trapped in a world of darkness and despair, seemingly trapped in an endless cycle of guilt, helplessness, and hopelessness, with no apparent way out of this life of misery.

Depression — Genetic Predisposition to Doom?

Today, modern science understands that genetics and neurochemistry play a primary role in Major Depressive Disorder and a large part in Bipolar Disorder, though the extent is still unknown. The age-old question of how much our personality is due to nature (genetics) and how much is nurture (learned or environmental) is still unresolved, though we know that nature and nurture are both important in determining who we are and how we function. Research has proven that biology does matter. There is growing evidence of a genetic predisposition to depression and of neurochemical factors that play a role in depression in both its onset and perpetuation. Unfortunately, as a therapist, too often I encounter clients who believe that their depressed mental state is 100% genetically determined or that there is a neurochemical imbalance in their brain or that they have no control over their depression. They are not correct.

That's the thing about depression: A human being can
survive almost anything, as long as she sees the end in
sight. But depression is so insidious, and it compounds
daily, that it's impossible to ever see the end. The fog is
like a cage without a key.

— *Elizabeth Wurtzel*

Unfortunately, feeling hopeless and helpless are major symptoms of depression, thus depressed people are prone to believe that it's useless to fight this hereditary trait and that their only hope is to be medicated.

Depression further perpetuates itself because depressed people are vulnerable to focusing on what they don't want and on what they fear, and to turning away from what they want. Their situation is similar to that of a person who stutters or one who is anxious about speaking. If people who stutter focus on not stuttering when they talk, they will stutter more. If nervous speakers focus on cues that they are nervous, such as perspiring or shaky hands, their cracking voice only serves to bring on more nervous reactions. A depressed person might focus on symptoms such as decreased energy; feeling sad, unhappy, hopeless, helpless, irritable, and/or empty; sleeping too much or too little; loss of interest in people and daily activities; preoccupation with death and dying; thoughts of suicide; and loss or increase in appetite.

In addition, depression can cause cognitive symptoms, such as negative or distorted thinking, difficulty concentrating, distractibility, forgetfulness, slower reaction time, memory loss, and indecisiveness.

In my opinion, when cognitive symptoms of depression
hit, they are more of a pressing concern than the
physical symptoms.

— *Dr. Deborah Serani, clinical psychologist and author*

As a result of reviewing all of the possible symptoms of depression, you probably have a better understanding of how depressed people can get trapped in a seemingly endless cycle of depression, in a mental state of despair, hopelessness, and helplessness. That's why they have a high rate of attempted suicide.

> What you perceive, your observations, feelings, interpretations, are all your truth. Your truth is important. Yet it is not *the* truth.
>
> — *Linda Ellinor*

As you are aware, knowledge is power. When you understand the facts about depression, you can empower yourself to defeat and take charge of this disabling disorder.

How Do You Fight Against a Possible Genetic Predisposition To Depression?

In my experience, overcoming genetically based depression is similar to overcoming a genetic predisposition to alcoholism or Attention-Deficit/Hyperactivity Disorder (ADHD).

Science presently contends that alcoholism is hereditary. It runs in families via a genetic predisposition. If you strictly adhere to this concept, children, especially male children, of alcoholics may as well throw in the towel because they are predestined to become alcoholics. In reality, although you may be predisposed to alcoholism, you are not fated to become an alcoholic. Even if you are genetically predisposed, you can do something to prevent or recover from alcoholism.

Undoubtedly, these children who have alcoholic genetics are at a higher risk to develop alcoholism. But if you educate yourself about alcoholism, you can make good choices and take positive and deliberate steps to avoid becoming an alcoholic. Many people successfully do this, whether or not alcoholism runs in their family.

The same scenario is true for ADHD. One of the major symptoms of this disorder is the inability to become organized. Again, knowledge is power, and most of my ADHD clients learn techniques and methods to become more organized.

And it's the same scenario for depression. When my depressed clients follow the principles I present in this book, they become empowered, knowledgeable, and proactive. They take deliberate steps to successfully fight and overcome their mental state of depression.

How Do You Fight Against Depressive Neurochemistry?

As I stated earlier in this book, it has been scientifically proven that our thoughts make chemicals that impact our lives, actually change our body chemistry, and rewire our brain's circuitry. In addition, when you have depressing or sad thoughts, your brain's limbic system induces clinical depression, irritability, lack of motivation, and sleep problems. Also, habitual negative thinking produces depression by causing unhealthy levels of various mood-maintaining neurochemicals.

Remarkable New Research Findings — Effects of Depression on the Body

> Depression can shrink your brain and shorten your life,
> while happiness is a tonic.
> — *Michael Lemmick,* Time *science writer*

Recent research indicates that depression is a systemic disorder and many of the neurotransmitters and chemicals that are involved in depression have serious negative implications throughout the body.[34]

The research suggests that untreated depression can have several serious consequences:

Heart disease: The heartbeat of people with depression usually is abnormally steady, which sounds beneficial. Ideally the healthy heart varies, which allows the heart to respond appropriately to various tasks as required. For example, while exercising the rate of heartbeats should increase.[35]

Diabetes: Depressed diabetics are more likely to suffer complications, including heart disease, nerve damage, and blindness. Also, depression makes the body less responsive to insulin.[36]

Arterial blood clots: Recent studies suggest that since depression lowers serotonin levels, it is a contributing factor to arterial blood clots.[37]

Among the serious conditions that these blood clots can cause are heart attacks and strokes.

Other diseases: Recent studies have established direct connections between depression and several other diseases, including cancer, stroke, Parkinson's disease, and Alzheimer's, though more research is needed to fully explain the possible connections.[38]

The Importance of Resiliency

We found that positive emotions are mild and subtle,
while negative emotions hit like a sledgehammer.
— *Dr. Barbara Fredrickson, psychologist and author*

Recent research indicates that people who are resilient tend to experience positive emotions along with their negative emotions. Without the presence of positive emotions to balance them, negative emotions make depression and anxiety more intense. Thus, people who are resilient are less intensely affected by depression and anxiety because their positive emotions offset their negative feelings.

Cognitive restructuring techniques such as reframing; *Boulder, Rock, and Pebble*; load shedding; and rebuttal of the ten cognitive distortions all work to improve your mental state.

As I said in Chapter 3, you can learn to increase your resiliency by exercise, meditation, and use of cognitive restructuring techniques. Diet may also play a role in increasing resiliency. In a recent study, Dr. Tamlin Conner found a strong relationship between a diet high in vegetables and fruits and having positive moods. At the present time, although it is not clear exactly why such a diet works, it appears such a diet may increase serotonin, one of the neurochemicals that prevents some forms of depression.[39]

Proven Method to Fight Depression

> You largely constructed your depression. It wasn't
> handed to you. Therefore, you can destruct it.
> — *Albert Ellis, psychologist and author*

Your Thoughts Affect Your Moods

Have you ever wondered why you become depressed? I would like
to give you a little test to help you analyze yourself.

The Thought-Analyzer Test[40]

1. When I am happy, I have been thinking _____ thoughts.
2. When I am sad, I have been thinking _____ thoughts.
3. When I am angry, I have been thinking _____ thoughts.
4. When I am depressed, I have been thinking _____ thoughts.

The answers are:
1. Happy
2. Sad
3. Angry
4. Depressing

This concept is so profoundly simple that it is simply profound —
the way we think will affect the moods we are in.

Over the years, I have successfully treated numerous depressed
clients. I have discovered that their self-defeating, irrational thinking
often revolves around the following cognitive themes:

- I must be perfect, or I am no good.
- I have failed more than the "average person."
- Because of my failing, I don't deserve love.
- I'm not worthy of happiness.
- I should have behaved differently.
- If someone criticizes me, there must be something wrong with me.

- I'm hopeless and destined to be depressed forever.
- Other people are responsible for my problem.

More than likely, these people formulated these self-deprecating, dysfunctional thought patterns as a result of how they were raised and/or from experiences acquired throughout life. Just because you think a certain negative thought does not mean that thought is based in reality. Just because you feel a certain negative way does not mean your feeling is based in reality. Most often, your negative thought or feeling is a reflection of a specific cognitive distortion, *emotional reasoning*. People construct their own reality and, too often, it is unrealistic. Your thoughts create your feelings and, if your thoughts are distorted, so are your feelings — and so is your reality. If your negative perception of yourself and your world is contrived by your negative thoughts, your distorted view permeates every aspect of your life. You *create* the quality and nature of your own life, existence, and future opportunities by the way you think. Your schema of you and your world is based upon how and what you *think*.

Always keep in mind the Law of Resistance: change the thought(s) that creates your resistance and there is no more resistance to living a peaceful, rewarding life. Also, make the Law of Association an integral theme in your life: thoughts attract like thoughts.

This book has introduced you to proven methods to stop dysfunctional, negative thinking in its tracks and to make rebuttals before irrational, self-defeating thought patterns can spiral you down into a vulnerable state of mind. Rebutting your negative thoughts changes your state of mind positively, to a state of mind that, with practice, you can control. Focus on what you want! Good thoughts attract more good thoughts, which bring good things into your life. Negative emotions, such as fear, despair, and sadness, are survival emotions. Positive emotions, such as hope and inspiration, help us thrive.

In the following account you will be amazed by how such a seemingly bright and promising young lady could be so tormented and so depressed. The techniques I showed her are techniques you can use, too, to deal with depression and the thoughts that cause it.

Andrea's Story

Andrea was barely 17 years old when she sought counseling for depression. She had one sibling, her 24-year-old sister. Her parents had been married for 26 years but had recently separated. Her father was an alcoholic and her mother recently forced her father to move out of the house, primarily due to his drinking problem — his drinking caused numerous conflicts and much distress and chaos in the household. When drinking, he would often get enraged and become verbally and sometimes physically abusive.

Andrea was a senior in high school. She was an excellent student and a good athlete. She planned on going to college and majoring in science.

During the initial sessions, I evaluated her for depression. I found her to be severely depressed. She reported several specific symptoms: She was so sad that she could not snap out of it. She felt hopeless, and she was extremely self-critical. She felt like a failure. She believed that she had no future. And she was becoming more and more socially isolated. I then asked Andrea an important question.

Do you limit your happiness? If so, how?

You may want to ask yourself the same question I usually ask at this point in counseling. I asked Andrea to completed this sentence: I limit my happiness by _____

Andrea's responses

- Not being worthy of happiness
- Not being good enough
- Feeling that my friends will abandon me

Her most disconcerting response was, "If my own father hates me, why should anyone else love me, and I don't deserve to be loved."

You might well ask, "How and why could such an attractive, athletic, talented student with so much going for her be so depressed?" The answer is that alcoholism often has devastating consequences on all family members, not just the alcoholic.

Children of Alcoholics

A few of the characteristics of adolescent or adult children of alcoholics that Andrea displayed included:

Fear of losing control

As a child, Andrea's environment was so chaotic that in her teens she needed to be in control so she would not experience those out-of-control feelings again. Andrea feared that her life would get worse if she lost control. She would become uncomfortable and anxious when she could not control situations, her feelings, and her behavior.

Fear of harsh criticism

Andrea feared criticism by others and was intensely self-critical because her father relentlessly criticized her when he was drunk.

Fear of abandonment

In order to avoid feeling abandoned, Andrea would do almost anything to hold on to a relationship.

Overdeveloped sense of responsibility

Andrea's self-esteem came from how others viewed her. She also had a compulsive need to be perfect though, in reality, nothing made her feel good enough.

Fear of failing

Andrea was obsessed with perfection because she was afraid of failing. She believed that if she failed, she would again be open to criticism. And even though she had a 3.8 cumulative grade point average and was a letter-winning athlete, her inner voice told her that she was never good enough and that she could never meet her father's expectations.

To add to her misery, Andrea became quite proficient at testing her dysfunctional assumptions regarding abandonment. She became a victim of a self-fulfilling prophecy whereby, even though she had a fear of abandonment, she would develop perfectly good relationships and then end them before, in her mind, the other person could abandon her. This experience would then serve to confirm her beliefs that "I don't deserve love. Everyone will abandon me." In my book, *Relationship Sabotage: Unconscious Factors That Destroy Couples, Marriages, and Family*, I explored in depth how unconsciously you can destroy relationships and people that you love. Andrea fit the pattern well.

At this point, I introduced Andrea to two cognitive restructuring techniques: *Examine the evidence* and *What would you say to a friend*.

Examine the evidence

To use this technique, ask yourself, what is the objective, factual evidence for a belief, for example, Andrea's belief that she could never be good enough? When pressed, her nonsensical responses seemed ludicrous. She had a 3.8 cumulative grade point average and was a good athlete. She was popular, likeable, and a person of high moral standards. Not good enough for whom? An alcoholic father who could barely keep a job. A pitiful person who lost his dignity and who lost his most precious loved ones, his children and his wife.

What would you say to a friend?

Another cognitive restructuring technique that I find helpful in jolting peoples' faulty thinking or misconceptions is to ask them what they would say in an imaginary scenario. During her counseling sessions, I asked Andrea to imagine that a close friend who has a problem was sitting across from her. I then asked Andrea what advice she would give to her imaginary friend. For example, what if the friend's problem was that her father hates her and why should anyone else love her? Or the friend feels that she doesn't deserve to be loved? Andrea initially replied, "She's not me." I responded, "She is you. Step outside yourself and really imagine your friend approaching you with a similar concern. Now what would you honestly say to her?"

Andrea replied, "I would drive home the point that she is not responsible for her father's self-hate, guilt, and his disgust with himself and the life he created. His behavior is irresponsible, child-like, and he lives in a world of denial."

I went on to discuss with Andrea that alcohol is a depressant and her father's constant need to escape reality by drinking only served to make him more depressed, which further fueled his drinking.

Projection and displacement

As part of the *What would you say to a friend?* technique, I explained to Andrea a defense mechanism, called projection or displacement, which everyone uses at times: We displace or project our intolerable feelings about ourselves onto others.

Whenever we have strong emotions trapped inside ourselves, such as frustration or anger, we may attempt to get rid of these tormenting feelings. For example, when we feel anger at ourselves, we may displace or project these angry feelings onto others. Frequently, children will act out their angry feelings by bullying others or getting into fights. Actually, they are angry with themselves, cannot tolerate that feeling, and cope with it by getting rid of it, by displacing it onto — or taking it out on — others.

Externalization

I also informed Andrea that in addition to projecting their unwanted feelings onto others, addicts often resort to *externalization* in a futile attempt to plausibly deny their addiction. Externalization means that they rationalize their inability to stop drinking or taking drugs by convincing themselves that they drink or take drugs to cope with their job, family, life circumstances, and/or stresses. An addicts' classic statement is, "If it weren't for…I would stop." "If it weren't for…" "If it weren't for…"

Again, I asked Andrea what she would tell a friend whose life was similar to hers. Andrea replied, "Your father's drinking has nothing to do with you. He's an addict who can't cope with life. He's projecting onto you qualities that he hates about himself. He's the loser, not you. You are lovable, people like you and admire you. You need to be your own advocate, and your own best friend. You can't rely on your father for love and support when he can't love himself."

Andrea learned that when you have the ability to look at things differently, you change the way you look at things. She gained an

enlightened,   more   realistic | **When you have the ability to look at things differently, you change the way you look at things.**
perception of her father and how his |
addictive behavior had affected her. |

Andrea then began to gain insight into how her reactions to her father, and her patterns of thinking, were self-deprecating and self-defeating for her mental well-being. More importantly, she realized that her depression was due to the irrational and addictive behavior of her *sick* father. She came to the conclusion that her dysfunctional, unwarranted thoughts were causing her resistance to positive change and thus were inhibiting her ability to live and enjoy her life — a purposeful life created in spite of not having a loving, nurturing father figure.

With practice, she was able to recognize the onslaught of negative thoughts before they could spiral her down into a state of despair (Law of Association). She utilized *Red Light/Green Light* to stop negative patterns of thinking in their tracks. Her initial, small success at rebutting faulty thinking eventually grew into an ability to take control of her thinking and emotional state (Law of Motivation). Andrea was no longer a prisoner of her dysfunctional way of thinking. She was liberated from her old, habitual thoughts and able to focus on what she wanted — and what she deserved from life. And her renewed enthusiasm and zest for life was contagious, serving to enhance her once-dismal social life.

Self-Destruction by Guilt

I encounter so many clients who are tormented by guilt. They seem to sentence themselves to a life of recrimination for past mistakes made in relationships. They constantly use *should haves* against themselves. We all make mistakes, and will continue to make mistakes — making mistakes is part of being human. Each mistake is water under the bridge, and all we can do is try to learn from our mistakes and move on.

Also, in my practice I have encountered people who were emotionally crippled by the *shouldn'ts*: "I shouldn't feel such happiness." "I should have reacted differently." "I should have told them I loved them more often." "I shouldn't put myself first." etc. The *should haves* and the *shouldn'ts* can be a form of self-punishment and guilt that can lead not only to depression but also to alcoholism, drug addiction, and even suicide.

Children who are severely guilt-ridden or unjustly accused of wrongdoing are often so incapable of living with guilt that they act out, become aggressive, or exhibit rebellious, antisocial, law-breaking behaviors, and/or drug and alcohol abuse. Conversely, they may succumb to their guilt and then feel worthless and undeserving, and display low self-esteem or depression. I have found that, unfortunately, children nearly always blame themselves for the break-up of their parents. They almost always believe that they should have somehow prevented the divorce.

> Guilt keeps you from doing what you want; and often keeps you a slave to someone else.
> — *Dr. Michael Mantell, psychologist and author*

Ironically, people often shower themselves with guilt because they feel comfortable with it, like the proverbial old shoe. Guilt may also be a means to feel loved — for some children, nagging is the closest thing to love that they ever receive. And for most people, bad attention is better than no attention — at least they can feel that they exist and have some sort of connection, however grim, to other people.

For some people, their dysfunctional guilt keeps them a slave to another person. Most feelings of guilt or shame stem from others demanding you do the right thing as they see it, a form of putting others before yourself. We cannot be responsible for how others react to us. We can only be responsible for our actions. Emotionally sound people must learn to develop the same tolerant goodwill and love toward themselves that they develop and feel towards their good friends and family.

Caring for Others

Caring for others brings us joy. Caring is one of the thriving emotions. Extending ourselves to others can give us pleasure. Giving to others is usually benevolent, but it can be destructive at times. Like most things in life, too much of a good thing can become problematic. Our good intentions may result in others taking advantage of us, in conflicting roles, and in unreasonable demands from unreasonable people. Frequently we may feel guilty if we don't respond to the needs of others. In my experience, when we feel overwhelmed and overextended, that usually is a signal that someone is taking advantage of our kindness. At times it is difficult to be responsible for our own state of affairs, let alone be responsible for the well-being of others. In reality, you need to take care of yourself first, to love yourself first, before you take care of others. It's the natural order of things.

When you feel resentful or overwhelmed, it indicates that your boundaries are becoming blurred and it may be time to put your own needs first. You may need to become more assertive and tell the other person what you need from the relationship. Maybe it's time to say no.

SOLUTION SUMMARY

- Both genes and the people we grow up with play a role in depression.
- Depression grows when we focus on it.
- Clearing out mistaken ideas is a way to stop depression, even if we have depression genes.
- Depression causes diseases, such as heart disease, and makes other diseases worse.
- Resiliency, being able to balance positive emotions against our negative emotions, reduces depression.
- The Four Laws and their techniques combat depression.
- *Examine the evidence* and *What would you say?* techniques can break the cycle of only looking inward.
- Children of alcoholics and other abusers are prone to depression and need to carefully check the messages they have been given. Under close examination, it's the abuser's self-hate that is being expressed, not truths about the child.
- Guilt can feel comfortable, but confronting it and moving on is a healthier way to live.

10. Taking Charge of Making a Better Marriage

Everyone could dramatically improve their marriage if
they only knew how.

—Dr. William Matta

For the past 22 years, a significant percentage of my practice has been devoted to marriage and couples counseling. In 2006, I published a book called *Relationship Sabotage: Unconscious Factors that Destroy Couples, Marriages, and Family.*

It may sound like a cliché, but without a doubt, the primary factor that determines if a marriage will survive is the ability to communicate in a healthy and effective manner. If a couple cannot communicate, in all likelihood their relationship is doomed to fail.

Marital Fights Should Not Mean Survival of the Fittest

I observe firsthand how couples can organize their disagreements into a "survival of the fittest" mode. This is especially true when the couples need to resolve serious, emotionally charged issues such as finances, distribution of chores, childrearing, in-law problems, and social activities.

Sometimes both persons feel that they own the truth, and they are going to prove they are right, no matter what! They continually lock themselves into verbal conflicts and outbursts, which only the fittest mate can survive. They lock themselves into a war of wills, wits, and words from which only one party will seemingly emerge victorious while the other party is seemingly defeated. Nevertheless, the damage has been done — and in reality, no one wins. The conquered mate stops fighting, and the important relational issues that disagreements are supposed to clarify never get addressed or resolved. The victor, or dominant aggressor in the struggle for power, becomes the master of the domain, but the relationship is fractured, shaky, shallow, and filled with resentment. As time goes by, the subservient party becomes more frustrated and angry, and the couple emotionally drifts apart. The dominant mate's attempt to control backfires.

> 67.5 % of divorce cases have a lack of communication in
> marriage as the driving factor.
>
> — *Abhijit Naik*

A marital fight can be viewed as an atomic explosion. Once the discussion evolves into all-out warfare, it causes such fallout that it takes hours, days, or even weeks to recover. Also, if you feel attacked, you only have two choices — fight or flight. You are then in survival mode. During these volatile moments, people often say things to their spouses that are cruel, spiteful, and anger driven. Once you say it, you can't take it back and, in my experience, people can forgive but rarely forget. No wonder the couple doesn't feel emotionally close, losing their connection and going through the motions.

I confess to my battling clients that I have been married for over forty years and, yes, my wife and I have had some heated discussions. But, when arguments escalate, the trick is to agree to take a time out — get away from each other until things settle down. It is imperative that you reinitiate the conversation as soon as you both feel comfortable again. It could take minutes, hours, or even possibly a few days, but you need to approach each other in a calm, productive fashion.

> 96% of the time, the first three minutes of a couple's
> dialogue predicts whether or not problem resolution
> will take place.
>
> — *Dr. John Gottman, psychologist and author*

Popular wisdom tells us that most men withdraw from conflict and difficult conversations, while most women pursue communication. The more the woman pursues, the more the man withdraws. The woman is perceived by the man as a nag, and the man is perceived as uncaring or apathetic. The couple then moves further and further apart, and problems are never resolved. Spouses need to learn how to approach each other and resolve their problems. All couples need to learn how to organize problem-solving conversations.

Couples who contend that they won't have problems or they shouldn't have marital issues will probably not survive. There will always be issues. There will always be problems. What is crucial for marital success is the willingness and ability to organize problem-solving conversations.

Organizing Problem-Solving Conversations

Instrumental in organizing problem-solving conversations is the attitude: *it's not so much what we say — it's how we say it.* For example, if I say to my wife, "You ticked me off again because you're late," guess where that's going? But if I say, "I feel hurt; I was disappointed that

> *It's not so much what we have to say — it's how we say it*

you were not on time," this softer approach is more conducive to further discussion and resolution. Again, it's not so much what we have to say — it's how we say it. In essence, you are sending a more constructive message than a destructive message. You must carefully choose your words.

I strongly suggest that you use the following steps to fair fighting when communicating with your spouse.

Rules for Fair Fighting

- The person who has the problem is responsible for bringing it up as soon as possible. Before you bring up the problem, think it through in your own mind.

- State the problem to your partner as clearly and concretely as possible. Use the format: "I am feeling... (for example, frustrated) because of..."
- It is important that you both understand the problem being brought up. The partner who is on the receiving end should reflect back what was said using the format: "I hear you saying you felt...because of..."
- When both partners agree on what is being said, the first partner may proceed.
- The partner who brings up the problem should take responsibility for offering a possible solution: "I would like to suggest..."
- This solution can be discussed, and then the other partner may offer a counter-proposal.
- Discuss several options until you agree that one proposal is more workable — not right or wrong but workable.
- Once you have agreed on a plan, proceed to talk about how you will put it into action. This means being able to clearly answer the questions: who will do what, when, and how?
- Now that you have reached an agreement, think about what could happen to undermine it. Who could sabotage this agreement, and how?
- Working through a conflict stirs up a lot of feelings and means you had to give up something. Congratulate each other for the hard work and willingness to compromise. Reaffirm your relationship in as many ways as possible. You have good reason to celebrate.
- Agree to come back to this problem after some specific period of time to reassess how the agreement is working. You may need to change it or fine-tune part of it.

Additional Suggestions for Constructive Conflict

In addition to these first eleven rules, here are some guidelines suggested by my clients themselves.

- Be specific when you introduce a gripe.
- Don't just complain, no matter how specifically. Ask for a reasonable change that will relieve one gripe.

- Do not use words such as *always* or *never*.
- Confine yourself to one issue at a time. Otherwise, without professional guidance, you may skip back and forth, evading the harder issues.
- Always consider compromise. Remember, your partner's view of reality feels just as real to him/her as yours does to you, even though you may differ. In relationships, there are no totally objective realities.
- Do not allow counter-demands to enter the picture until the original demands are clearly understood and there has been a clear-cut response to them.
- Never assume that you know what your partner is thinking or predict how s/he will react or what s/he will accept or reject until you have checked out your assumption in plain language with your partner.
- Never put labels on a partner. Call him/her neither a coward, nor a neurotic, nor a child. If you really believed that s/he is incompetent or suffers from some basic flaw, you probably would not be with her/him. Do not make sweeping, labeling judgments about any of your partner's feelings.
- Sarcasm is dirty fighting.
- Forget the past, and stay with the here and now. What either of you did last year or last month or that morning is not as important as what you are doing and feeling now. The changes you are asking for cannot possibly be retroactive. Hurts, grievances, and irritations should be brought up at the very earliest moment, or else the partner has the right to suspect that they may have been saved carefully as weapons.
- Meditate. Take time to consult your real thoughts and feelings before speaking. Your surface reactions may mask something deeper and more important. Don't be afraid to ask your partner for some time to think.

Additional key guidelines for the speaker and the listener to follow are contained in Appendix A.

If you make a commitment to practice and consistently utilize these rules, especially for emotional or sensitive issues, you are on the right course towards resolving relationship issues.

Being Courteous

> Common courtesy plays a big role in happy marriages. People who are permanently married are polite to one another. They don't want to hurt one another's feelings, and they don't try to make the other one feel humiliated. People who are married for life are extremely kind to one another.
>
> — *Dr. Frank Pitman, psychiatrist and author*

I find that when couples are courteous to each other and understand the importance of validating each other, communication progresses smoothly. All of us want and need to be validated, and not taken for granted. The speaker must view the interaction as important and the listener must be attentive, open, and responsive. Keep in mind that being validated in your married life is as important as being validated in your work or personal life. If our feelings are not validated, we become frustrated, angry, and even aggressive with our partner.

Eventually the partners become more and more isolated, doing their own thing. Frequently, discussions will escalate into a full-blown altercation in which we scream at each other in a futile attempt to be heard. When we perceive the event to be a threat, we activate the emergency part of our nervous system — fight or flight and the survival emotions — and thus we retreat, withdraw, or attack. Aggressive behavior and resentments can be avoided by organizing problem-solving conversations, as well as having the willingness and ability to compromise.

I find that one of the most frustrating counseling scenarios occurs when one of the spouses feels that they own the truth and there is

> *We don't see things as they are; we see things as we are.*

no room for compromise. Each of us sees the world through the filter or lens of our own desires, preferences, values, upbringing, and past experiences. One person's view represents only one perspective of truth or reality. We don't see things as they are; we see things as we are. In my estimation, marriage is compromise, compromise, compromise.

Getting What You Want In Your Marriage

Earlier, I briefly discussed the necessity, and even obligation, of telling the other partner what you need that you are not getting. This concept is crucial for effective communication and validation of one's feelings. If couples would follow this rule, there would be no need to second-guess what the partner wants and needs. Often I observe couples playing a psychological game using double-bind messages where one partner feel damned if you do and damned if you don't.

Double-bind messages

Double-bind messages are a set of contradictory messages from a partner to which the spouse is expected to respond although his/her failure to please is inevitable. No matter what response is given, double binds sabotage fair play and honest communication, and block intimacy and a sense of closeness. A few of the double-bind messages that I hear couples give are:

- "If you loved me, you would know what I want."
- "By now, you should know that..."
- "I know what you want; you should know what I want."
- "If you took the time to understand me, you would know that..."
- "After all these years you should know that..."

How to Properly Ask for What You Want

A successful technique I have used over the years looks at how to properly ask for what you want. This format enhances intimacy, connection, and validation for each person. The procedure, borrowed from Robert Sherman and Norman Freedman,[41] has three aspects. Each person must identify clearly and specifically what he or she wants. The wants must be stated as a desire for something that will happen, not as a desire for something not happening. Each partner should surprise the other regularly with positive behaviors.

When couples utilize this technique, they take responsibility for change and for becoming more accountable for happiness in the relationship.

You Cannot Make Others Change Except by Changing Yourself

> When we change, it changes the way we view things,
> and the things we view change.
>
> — *Unknown*

A major factor in facilitating healthy and effective communication is attitude. I find that at the start of counseling, many couples feel defeated. They feel that their relations are hopeless, and they feel helpless, believing that no matter what they do, nothing will change. However, the truth of the matter is that we have more control and power than we realize. Recall the story in Chapter 2 about how I met the challenge of teaching a late-Friday class. Just as my purposefully and consciously projected enthusiasm energized the students, the same sort of scenario can work in couples. If you want your spouse to change, you change. If you want your spouse to be more considerate, you be more considerate. In fact, I'm convinced that what we try to control in a spouse actually backfires. If we want people to change, we must change. When we change, it changes the way we view things, and the things we view change.

The Secret to a Happy, Flourishing Marriage

During the first marriage-counseling session, I make it emphatically clear to the couple that, generally speaking, I don't take sides — except with the relationship. I'm not here to allow one partner to expand upon how the other partner is responsible for the problems with the marriage. I make exceptions only for substance abuse, physical or sexual abuse, or severe emotional abuse, and also for affairs. I also tell the couple that in general both partners are responsible for the couple's problems and therefore both are responsible for the solution. Eventually, as the sessions progress, I inform them that the secret to a happy relationship is to think in terms of marital best interest.

Think in Terms of Marital Best Interest

> Thinking in terms of marital best interest, in my estimation, would virtually eliminate divorce.
> — *Dr. William Matta*

If couples would practice always putting the relationship first, everything — and I mean every issue, every problem — would solve itself. If every couple followed the principles that I thus far have described — carefully selecting your words when talking to your partner, organizing problem-solving-conversations, clearly telling your partner what you need and are not getting in the relationship, thinking in terms of marital best interest, to name a few — divorce attorneys would be put out of business.

Thinking in terms of marital best interest needs to be the reference point for every possible issue, problem, or situation that could possibly affect your marital relationship — in-law problems, chores and household responsibilities, social activities, financial issues, childrearing, going out with your own friends, where to spend the holidays, date nights, etc. Put your relationship first, always!

> Marriage is an attempt to solve problems together, which you didn't even have when you were on your own.
> — *Eddie Cantor, comedian*

Difficult scenarios for couples

I have found two scenarios that are especially difficult for couples to navigate — the birth of biological children and dealing with stepchildren.

Birth of a biological child

The top priority when a child is born, especially for the mother, is to nurture and take care of the newborn. There is nothing in life more special than the loving and caring relationship between a mother and her child. It is easy for a couple to devote almost 100% of their time to the child, thus inadvertently putting marital best interest second and neglecting or taking for granted the need to nurture and cherish the couple's relationship.

Couples who have become new parents are entering uncharted waters that are difficult to navigate. It takes a lot of constructive messages and conversations to navigate these tricky waters successfully. Often we stop putting our partners first, and we stop doing things as a couple. We may do things as a family, but we also need to do things as a couple. Couples need to get away from the children occasionally and take care of each other.

As a family therapist, I tell people that any discord between the spouses will reverberate throughout the family. The husband and wife must take care of each other for the children to feel secure and nurtured. Quite often, the family's relational arrangement is dysfunctional in that the children always come first. If a healthy family is to flourish, it is imperative that the spouses first need to take care of each other — and, as a result, the children's emotional needs will be met.

Dealing with Stepchildren: Blended Families Have Unique Marital Problems

The divorce rate for blended families approaches 70%.

— U.S. statistics

The second situation which couples often have a difficult time negotiating is dealing with stepchildren in a blended family or stepfamily.

From the time of the marriage, stepfamilies have numerous potentially serious issues that must be navigated. If the marriage is going to succeed, the couple must make a firm commitment to the marriage, have a strong emotional bond to each other, think in terms of marital best interest, and — most importantly — organize problem-solving conversations.

In all likelihood, the couple in a stepfamily will be bombarded from many directions. Some people involved in the relationship will have a vested interest in the marriage failing. A major reason why the failure rate approaches seventy percent is because often the children sabotage the relationship. There are rough seas ahead for the couple because undermining forces, besides the children, may include the ex-spouses and the spouses themselves.

The problems may include the resentment the children feel regarding the divorce and the remarriage. The children undermine the authority of the new marital arrangement. The children may also resent it when the natural parent and stepparent produce their own children. Other issues arise when the ex and the blended family have different sets of rules. Also, in many cases the child is oppositional and hesitant about treating the stepmother or stepfather as a parent figure. And frequently when the children become teenagers, they manipulate the resident parents and threaten to leave and live with the natural parent.

Difficulties may arise when the children spend time with the ex and the ex uses these opportunities to befriend the children rather than parent them. If the ex is bitter about the divorce, s/he may deliberately undermine the ex-spouse's authority. Problems also surface when the ex complains and then the children relay complaints and criticisms to the other parent.

Couples' issues often arise in blended families when, for example, the stepparent attempts to become a parent figure to their stepchildren too soon in the relationship. The stepparent feels jealous because s/he perceives the spouse and his/her ex to be too friendly with each other or the stepparent becomes too involved in disciplining the stepchildren.

Sometimes ill feelings arise when the stepparent isn't as emotionally close to the stepchildren as is the biological parent.

My secretary told me a story about her husband Richard whose natural mother died when he was fifteen. Two years later his father remarried and the stepmother wanted the children to call her "Mom." Richard explained that he only had one mother and he would agree to call his stepmother anything else but he refused to call her "Mom." From that time until he moved out, Richard's life was affected by his stepmother's retaliation. Although he moved into an apartment of his own after he turned eighteen, his stepmother continued to resent him, and often she would take the opportunity to make life difficult for him or sabotage Richard's relationship with his father.

Richard's stepmother also erased everything in the home that was a reminder of Richard's mother, right down to the shrine his baby sister created in honor of her mother. With one sweep of her arm, the stepmother tossed it into the trashcan, remarking that the child's mother is not here anymore.

I'm sure there are other issues that blended families encounter, but I think you get the picture, especially if you are experiencing them yourself. Due to the complexity of the various dynamics in a blended family, the issues and problems can be daunting and volatile.

A marriage with a blended family can only succeed if the couple makes a firm commitment to the marriage, has a strong emotional bond to each other, thinks in terms of marital best interest, puts each other first, and, most definitely, organizes problem-solving conversations. Appendix B contains additional strategies for blended families. In Chapter 11, I will provide more advice regarding raising children in a blended family.

Intimacy versus Falling Out of Love

The level of intimacy depends on the level of mutual self-disclosure; the kind of intimate relationship we establish depends on the expression which we give to our self-disclosure.

– Author unknown

In an intimate relationship you never want to harm, manipulate, or try to convince the other of anything beyond what you believe is good for that person. Many couples whom I counsel feel isolated and distant from one another. They feel lonely, as if no one cares for them. They don't feel emotionally close to one another, and they have lost their intimacy. Intimacy refers to a sense of feeling close and connected and having a sense of warm-heartedness for the other. It also encompasses sharing oneself, giving and receiving emotional support, and trusting the spouse.

Triangular Theory of Love

Consider Sternberg's triangular theory of love, shown below. According to Sternberg, enduring love does not start with passionate romance. It starts with commitment to the development of a relationship. This commitment leads to intimacy, which in turn fuels passion. The passion serves to intensify commitment to the relationship, and intimacy and passions continue to nurture love.[42]

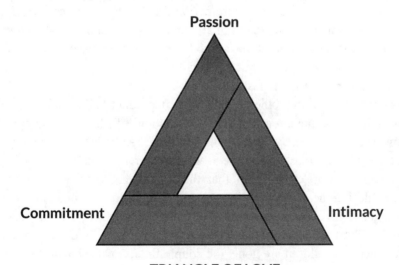

TRIANGLE OF LOVE

Commitment

In my practice, during the initial stages of counseling I ask the couple to establish an equal commitment to each other. Questions I ask in the session include "What is your definition of commitment?" "What would it take for you to be satisfied in your relationship?" "How invested are you in this relationship?"

Intimacy

Intimacy arises from the fusing and counterpointing, the dance of personalities. Intimacy is the ability to enter into concrete affiliations with others and the ethical strength to abide by those commitments. In my opinion, people often confuse the concepts of intimacy and infatuation and often comment that they have lost their intimacy in the relationship. Intimacy is different from infatuation.

Infatuation is the first stage of love. When we are first attracted to another, we become infatuated with that person. We see only the good in the person and do not see his or her faults. We put the person on a pedestal. When people have extramarital affairs, they become infatuated with the person and operate out of an unrealistic perception of the other. I often say that having an affair is like temporary insanity. Infatuation can last weeks or even years, but eventually it fades away and we see the person in a more realistic fashion.

Intimacy, on the other hand, is a byproduct of communication. Appendix C contains a detailed description of the components of intimacy, as outlined by Dr. Luciano L'Abate.[43] Although it is no surprise that the highest rate of divorce is in the first two years of marriage, people are surprised to learn that the second highest rate of divorce occurs during the empty-nest stage, when the children become adults and leave the house. The culprit is lack of communication. In my experience, roughly 80% of a couple's conversations revolve around the children, and when the children are gone, the couple finally realizes that they have lost their identity as a couple and that they have become less intimate. You become intimate by having honest, open conversations. As the years go by, if the couple does not work at validating each other by communicating about their relational needs and expectations, they grow farther and farther apart, and they lose their identity as a couple.

Intimacy is possible only after you have known a person long enough that you can affirm him or her realistically because of your appreciation of that person's gifts. The affirmed person knows that for the time being the affirming person regards him/her as the most important person there is. But the assumption is that after this moment both will carry on independently.

Over the years, people get lost in their parenting responsibilities, jobs, hobbies, and clubs. I tell people that we have to take our spouses more seriously than our jobs and hobbies. We have to treat our spouses as real people. We have to learn to work at a marriage. We have to work at validating the other, developing more sensitivity, and changing some priorities — or simply learning how to listen to one another. Couples need to understand that their behaviors influence their relationship. Their behaviors can make the relationship supportive or stressful.

Passion

The third component of the love triangle is passion. Passion is the romantic, physical, and sexual aspect of the relationship. It is the natural result of intimacy and commitment.

Falling Out of Love

I'd be rich if I had a penny for every time I've heard, "I like him/her but I don't love him/her." And when I question the speaker, unless they are having an affair, they find it extremely difficult to explain that statement.

Marriage thrives on intimacy and mutual emotional closeness. When intimacy declines, couples no longer feel in love with their spouse, even though they still care for and love their spouse.

How to Prevent Falling Out of Love

So, what does falling out of love mean? It doesn't mean infatuation, because infatuation is a state in which hormones are released in the brain.

That only lasts for six months to a year or so. If you want to bring back similar feelings, you can do so by reigniting feelings of intimacy.

You can bring excitement and passion back into your marriage, but it takes conscious effort and a cognitive shift. You need to go from needing excitement for yourself to creating excitement in your marriage for both of you. As you change, your partner will change. When you focus on the good things in your marriage, you feel good, you attract more positive thoughts, and good things will happen in your marriage.

Also, if you focus on the good in your marriage, you will be less tempted to start an affair — stepping outside of your marriage is not a good way to solve your marital problems.

So, make a commitment to work on your marriage. Respect and befriend your partner. Resolve conflict in a peaceful way. Show trust and concern about each other's welfare. Focus on your daily lives and the needs of your children.

Daily Affirmations: The Three A's

On a daily basis, use the three A's: affirmation, appreciation, and affection.

- Affirmation: "I like your nature." "I'm glad I married you." "I like being with you."
- Appreciation: "I appreciate you for all of you." "I like it when you smile."
- Affection: touching, kissing, holding, and making verbal statements of affection.

Forgiveness

Forgiveness is a natural outgrowth of love.
— *Dr. William Matta*

No one, including you, is perfect. Everyone makes mistakes. Everyone at times is angry, impatient, or inconsiderate. Intimacy is cultivated and grows from mutual tolerance. Loving your spouse in the light of imperfections allows you to love others even with all of their imperfections. Forgiveness is a natural outgrowth of love.

Resentment is a useless pursuit. No one wins. It doesn't help the situation and it doesn't help the relationship. Bad thoughts beget more bad thoughts and feelings that contribute to more ill feelings and further emotional distancing. Resentment often leads to volatile behavior within the relationship.

In a healthy relationship you have the right to talk about anything, including grievances. With forgiveness as a goal, you need to discuss grievances. You must let your spouse know how their action hurt you. Using the techniques that I previously presented in this chapter, the offense must be clearly presented to your spouse.

Forgiveness means that we rebut the thought that the offender is bad or evil, because the offender, like you, is only human.

Forgiveness does not mean making excuses for the offender or saying that what s/he did is somehow right. Forgiveness does not throw out accountability. By forgiving your spouse, you are choosing to focus on love and what is good about your marriage.

Forgiveness releases you from the anchor of resentment and frees you to move forward. Marriages have numerous opportunities for holding grudges, but there is little to be gained and a lot to lose from not letting go of resentments. Instead, focus on the good things about your marriage.

Right now, in your journal, write down the good things in your marriage and refer to them as needed.

Live the Law of Attraction — when you feel grateful for the privilege of having each other and focus on your love, pleasures, and joy, you enhance your emotional connection. In this state of mind, you can easily reframe, and minor grievances will be just that — minor pebbles in the sand.

Irv and Kayley Solve Their Marital Problems

Irv, age 44, and Kayley, age 40, entered counseling because they were arguing constantly. Married for 16 years, they had two children, Melissa, age 14, and Tyler, age 11. As I always do during the initial interview, I explained to Irv and Kayley that I take the side of the relationship and, even though marriage counseling can involve many layers, a primary goal of the process is improving how the couple organizes the space between themselves, how they go about solving issues, and their ability to organize problem-solving conversations. I emphasized the need to send constructive messages rather than destructive messages to each other. I reinforced how important it is to carefully choose words, and that what we say is not as important as how we say it. Last, I emphasized the importance of the first three minutes of a conversation and that if the conversation escalates, to take a break and stop the discussion by mutual agreement so that one doesn't feel that the other is walking away or leaving in disgust and anger. I then proceeded to ask for each partner's version of the major problems in the marriage.

Kayley reported that because Irv is consumed with his sales position, they don't spend enough time together; he doesn't seem to listen to her when she wants to discuss issues; and she needs more help around the house because she also works, as a beautician. Irv said that he realizes that he doesn't do enough around the house because his work frequently takes him out of town; he is too busy to go out with her without the children; and he also feels that she doesn't listen to him.

It became obvious that Irv and Kayley would drift further and further apart if they didn't make some changes. The potentially redeeming factor was that both emphatically stated their commitment to make the marriage work. I then explained the importance of the love triangle: commitment, intimacy, and passion. Again, both agreed that they had too much to lose and were willing to undertake a difficult journey in hopes of saving their marriage. Incidentally, when one spouse says s/he has no commitment to the marriage or to marriage counseling, I suspect that s/he may be having an affair, especially when I also hear "I love him/her, but I am not in love with him/her." In the face of such apparent lack of good faith, I do not provide further counseling sessions.

During the second session, all fury broke loose as they were discussing how both felt taken for granted and not validated. The argument briefly devolved into a screaming match which I naturally interrupted to ask if this volatile interaction was typical of the way they organized problem-solving conversations. Kayley said, "Yes, especially when Irv withdraws and shuts down." I then explained four vital points:

Four Vital Points about Marital Interactions

- In many marriages, the couple organizes the space between themselves by one person, usually the man, withdrawing during emotionally charged issues, and the other person, often the woman, pursuing. As a result, the man is perceived as not caring and the woman is perceived as a nag, resulting in a tendency to avoid discussing critical issues, which leads to emotional distance.
- Volatile interactions also result in emotional distance between the spouses and increase resentment.
- When conversations get out of control, each partner feels more invalidated and lonely.
- They need to learn more effective and productive ways to solve their marital issues.

During subsequent sessions, I discussed the topics outlined in this chapter: the fallout from volatile discussions; marital fights should not be the survival of the fittest; the necessity of organizing problem-solving conversations; steps to fair fighting; following good speaker-listener rules; your right to tell the other person what you need and are not getting; positive affirmations; thinking in terms of marital best interest; and how intimacy and forgiveness complement each other.

Kayley's and Irv's Dysfunctional Thinking Process

An integral part of the therapy focused on the absolute power of their thoughts and thinking patterns. It became clear that Kayley's dysfunctional thoughts blocked her ability to compromise and work on her marriage. For your convenience, the ten cognitive distortions are listed in Appendix D.

Kayley's dysfunctional thoughts

THOUGHT: "He never listens to me."
COGNITIVE DISTORTIONS: All-or-none thinking. Overgeneralization. Jumping to conclusions (fortune-telling and mind-reading). Personalization and blame.

THOUGHT: "It's too late. He will never change."
COGNITIVE DISTORTIONS: All-or-none thinking. Overgeneralization. Jumping to conclusions (fortune-telling).

THOUGHT: "It's obvious he doesn't care about me."
COGNITIVE DISTORTIONS: All-or-none thinking. Overgeneralization. Mental filter. Magnification.

THOUGHT: "After sixteen years of marriage, he should know what I want by now."
COGNITIVE DISTORTIONS: Jumping to conclusions (mind-reading). *Should* statements.

Irv's dysfunctional thoughts

THOUGHT: "It's always her way or the highway."
COGNITIVE DISTORTIONS: All-or-none thinking. Overgeneralization. Jumping to conclusions (fortune-telling).

THOUGHT: "She never listens to me."
COGNITIVE DISTORTIONS: All-or-none thinking. Overgeneralization. Jumping to conclusions (fortune-telling). Magnification. Personalization and blame.

THOUGHT: "No matter what I do, it's never enough."
COGNITIVE DISTORTIONS: All-or-none thinking. Overgeneralization. Mental filter. Magnification. Jumping to conclusions (fortune-telling).

THOUGHT: "She only cares about the children."

COGNITIVE DISTORTIONS: All-or-none thinking. Overgeneralization. Mental filter. Jumping to conclusions (mind-reading).

Kayley and Irv were surprised and enlightened by how their faulty thinking contributed to their negative feelings of resentment, frustration, anger, and loneliness. They became quite good at using reframing, cognitive rebuttals, and *Boulders, Rocks, and Pebbles* to transform their view of their marital arrangement.

Kayley's and Irv's Enlightened Thinking Process

In the service of marital best interest, they changed their internal self-talk:

FROM: "S/he never listens to me."
TO: "During the first years of our marriage we made the time to listen to each other. We really both want to be validated."

FROM: "It's too late. S/he will never change."
TO: "We need to have goodwill and faith in each other to navigate the changes in our lives. We both must be willing to give and take."

FROM: "It's obvious he doesn't care about me." and "She only cares about the children."
TO: "We need to think more in terms of marital best interest, put each other first, and have date nights."

FROM: "After sixteen years of marriage, he should know what I want."
TO: "I will no longer use communication double binds. Irv is also overwhelmed with work, but we need to sit down and, for example, calmly discuss redistributing the chore responsibility."

FROM: "It's always her way or the highway."
TO: "She has always been reasonable and open to discussion. Now I understand how important it is to really listen to what she needs. I'm

sure if I become more receptive to her, she'll become more willing to listen to me."

FROM: "No matter what I do, it's never good enough."
TO: "She's just reacting to her frustration, to my past unwillingness to appreciate all the things she does — she's overwhelmed. From now on I vow to practice daily the three A's — affirmation, appreciation and affection, as Dr. Matta requested that we do. I now realize we can't make others change; and now I see because it is working. When I change for the better, Kayley changes, too."

I then introduced Kayley and Irv to the *Red Light/Green Light* technique as applied to relationships and rehearsed it with them.

Red Light/Green Light Technique for Relationships

This mindfulness technique is a means for changing habitual emotional reactions that sabotage relationships. Each time you experience a negative emotion — for example, impatience, anger, disrespect, disloyalty, unfairness, lack of validation or appreciation — do the following:

Red Light/Green Light Technique

Red Light Mode

When you feel uncomfortable, disrespected, unappreciated, not validated, angry, etc., you enter the red light mode. In this mode, you stop reasoning and you simply react and even overreact.

STOP!

Breathe deeply, inhaling for four seconds and exhaling for eight seconds. Let yourself become calm. Pay attention to now. Allow the negative emotions to soften.

Yellow Light Mode

Appraise the situation:

THINK!

- What is my old pattern here?
- What is my reaction calling me to work on?
- Reframe a threat to a challenge.
- Use *Boulders, Rocks, & Pebbles.*
- In terms of marital best interest, how should I act?

Green Light Mode

- Take purposeful action. When you are reactivating the common sense, reasoning part of your brain — the frontal lobe —you are in a better place and you are more able to act, not just react.
- What is my best choice under the circumstances?
- Make a decision and a plan to implement it.

GO!

Congratulate yourself for a job well done. You have activated your emotional-reset button! Remember, just as you were conditioned to stop at a red light, with practice and rehearsal you will become conditioned to easily use this technique. You will not just react — you will purposefully act.

SOLUTION SUMMARY

- You have the power to create a better marriage.
- Marital fights should not be survival of the fittest.
- You can successfully organize problem-solving conversations.
- Fair fighting leads to solved problems and loving relationships.
- You can have what you want in your marriage.
- You can ask for what you need in a relationship.
- You can't make your partner change unless you change.
- The secret to a happy, flourishing marriage is thinking in terms of marital best interest.

- Blended families can solve their unique marital problems.
- You can fall back into love if you try.
- The triangle of love goes from commitment to intimacy to passion.
- Forgiveness is required for a healthy relationship.
- The *Red Light/Green Light* technique is a way to handle the overreactions that arise from negative emotions.

11. Taking Charge of Your Children

> The terrifying roars of dinosaurs and adolescents have a lot in common. Parents trying to set boundaries for teenagers can feel like the nervous gatekeepers of Jurassic Park.
>
> — *Ed Igle, Licensed Clinical Social Worker*

Teens often look bigger to their parents than they do to themselves. Just like dinosaurs testing the boundaries of the park perimeter in the movie *Jurassic Park*, teens test parental boundaries. It is part of their normal maturation process to challenge parental authority. If they didn't revolt — hopefully in a socially acceptable manner — they would not eventually detach from their parents and move on to become independent adults. Parents that do not take this revolt personally are more able to view this challenging behavior as part of the adolescent's normal growth process and see it as part of what it takes to raise a child. The adolescent's "temporary insanity" — irrational behavior — becomes more tolerable. Thus, the parent is less likely to overreact and more able to rationally discuss their teen's oppositional antics and continue to establish and reinforce boundaries.

The Single-Parent Paradox

If a couple divorces, the children often reside with their mother. Especially if the children are young, the child and the mother provide emotional support for each other. This close emotional arrangement benefits the mother and child until the child enters puberty. At that time, parental rules and boundaries may become blurred. What started out with good intentions as a loving and caring relationship often paradoxically transforms into unruly, aggressive behavior on the part of the teen.

Pam, a 42-year-old single mother, brought her 12-year-old son Anthony in for counseling. He was not a problem to his eighth grade teachers, but was often insulting, angry, and physically aggressive to his mother. Pam could not understand why the child that she adored was so disrespectful and mean to her. After all, she took care of him when his father abandoned the family when Anthony was five years old.

Although Anthony's father deserted the family, Pam felt guilty about Anthony not having a father figure, even though his uncles spent a lot of time with Anthony. Pam realized that she and Anthony had become more and more emotionally enmeshed while giving emotional support to each other. All went well until Anthony became an adolescent — time for Pam to act as a parent and set rules with natural, logical consequences for Anthony to follow.

She tried to set rules but he wouldn't listen to her. The mistake she made was typical: a parent gives emotional support to a child but does not expect to receive it in exchange, or else the relationship becomes too emotionally involved and enmeshed.

> Many working mothers feel guilty about not being at home. And when they are there, they wish it could be perfect. This pressure to make every minute happy puts working parents in a bind when it comes to setting limits and modifying behavior.
>
> — *Cathy Rindner Temelsman*

Single mothers often feel guilty about having to work and not being at home as much as they would like. Others feel guilty that the father figure is absent, or they fear temporary loss of approval from their child. What I encounter in counseling is that when the child becomes an adolescent, he tends to want what he wants by any means. The child often becomes a master at creating guilt trips, for example telling the mother, "It's your fault I don't have a Dad." "I hate you, no wonder Dad left." "I'm going to live with my Dad." "No one loves you, and why do you have to work? Tammy's Mom doesn't work." As a result of such faulty thinking, Mom feels guilty and the teen gets his or her way.

In extreme cases, the child acts as the parent. In these scenarios the teen decides everything, from what the family eats to when, if ever, homework gets done, when to go to school, and when to come home at night.

> The agenda of the adolescent is to reform the parent.
>
> — *Unknown*

Adolescence is a difficult and emotional time. Most teens don't have the experience and critical thinking skills to make consistently good choices. Actually, their brains are still growing and maturing, which continues until about age twenty-four. Teens are naturally self-centered and impulsive; they feel indestructible and take many risks. Teenagers glory in their newfound ability to formulate intellectual hypotheses, and they are constantly testing family values, rituals, rules, and standards. They become emotional philosophers and social critics, bringing what they perceive as new data to their parents and challenging the most heavily defended values and assumptions of the family. A new identity, not just a new body, is coming to life.

To all parents, and especially to single parents, their adolescent's looks are imposing, as they are often the size of an adult. Too often the single parent becomes too permissive, loses control due to guilt, drops any investment in setting boundaries, and abandons their teen to his/her own shabby ways.

> Dysfunctional families follow dysfunctional rules.
>
> – *Dr. William Matta*

Dysfunctional families follow dysfunctional rules. Rules define the relationship. Either the parents are in charge or the children are in charge — and the children cannot be in charge. In a fully functional family, the vast majority of a child's negative behavior can be resolved. However, some adolescent behaviors, for example pregnancy or committing a felony, can have long-term consequences. It is our duty as parents to help ensure that our adolescents' behaviors do not result in irresolvable predicaments such as law breaking and even homicide.

Parents, and especially single parents, must learn to play a nurturing yet firm role in establishing consistent rules with natural, logical consequences. Such rules and consequences modify unacceptable behavior and increase the odds that the child and, later, the teen will safely become a responsible adult. Developmentally speaking, parents must be in charge because adolescents are not ready to govern themselves. Often, in a joking way I tell the parent(s) of an adolescent that adolescents are "temporarily schizophrenic but eventually outgrow it."

Natural, logical consequences are discernibly different from punishment. Punishment takes place in the past tense. It is punitive, threatening, and rarely related to the misbehavior. And, usually at the time of the misbehavior, parents tend to get angry and blurt out an outlandish punishment, laden with unconscious resentments and fears, that is impossible to carry out. For example, the parent might say, "You failed algebra, and you are grounded for the remainder of the school year." This punishment is purely irrational, self-punishing, places too much of the responsibility for enforcement on the parent, and denies the child the opportunity to make his/her own decisions and take responsibility for his/her own behavior.

On the other hand, natural, logical consequences teach children to become more responsible. They teach children to be accountable for their own actions and choices. In my experience, a child is never too young to learn to be accountable. Natural, logical consequences permit children to learn from the natural order of things. For example, if you speed when driving, you can get a ticket. Rules with natural, logical consequences should be age appropriate. The rules for a 16 year old should be different from those for a 12 year old.

The parents who seem to do best with the challenges of adolescents are the ones that do not take their teenager's questions and attempts to reform the parents personally. Instead, they view this as part of what it takes to raise children who have minds of their own. These parents maintain an authoritative posture, working toward dialogue about why they hold the values they hold and how the values have been formed from concrete experience. However, both sides know that this dialogue is not going to lead to a dramatic organization change. The parent needs to be in charge, because developmentally the child is not ready for self-governing. Parents often make the mistake of trying to be their child's friend. They want the child to like them, but it is much more important that children respect their parents.

> If there is anything we wish to change in the child, we
> should first examine it and see whether it is not
> something that could be changed in ourselves.
>
> *– Carl Jung*

Throughout this chapter, I have made reference to a number of negative self-defeating and sabotaging thoughts, such as, "My son doesn't have a father." "I should take it easy on him. If I didn't have to work he would be a better kid." or "He has the right to act out. It's always my fault."

A Single-Parent Family: Adele

A typical single-parent scenario is provided by the Kanton family — 40 year old, single mother Adele and her 15-year-old daughter Tammy. Adele and Tammy's father divorced 12 years ago, after he left Adele for another woman. After the divorce he did not see Tammy for five years, and, even though he and his new wife lived close by, he only occasionally communicated with Tammy by e-mail. Adele and her ex have not talked to each other for years. As far as Adele was concerned, their relationship had been severed a long time ago.

During the first counseling session, Adele and Tammy agreed that Tammy was spoiled and manipulative. For example, if her mother wanted her home at 11:00 PM on a Saturday night, Tammy would sometimes stay out until 2:00 AM. And if her mother drew the line in an attempt to discipline her, Tammy would call her father for support and would relay his derogatory comments back to her mother.

Adele was a teacher and she made a good income. She was dating Carl and they intended to get married in the near future. Carl and Tammy tended to get along, and she didn't object to him being a future stepfather. Tammy claimed she had tried marijuana, but she hadn't used it for months. Tammy was a good student and wanted to be a lawyer.

By observing the interactions between Adele and Tammy in family sessions, it was obvious that Adele was not in charge. The relationship was enmeshed and the boundaries were blurred. At age 15, Tammy was attempting to establish herself as an independent adult. Adele needed to establish a more delineated parent-child boundary. It was imperative for Adele, as a mother, to set and enforce firm rules and consequences for her daughter to follow.

My treatment plan was to empower Adele, to place her in charge of the family. Adele needed assistance in establishing firmer limits. I intended to encourage her to revise her unworkable child-rearing patterns and become confident in building new patterns. Adele also needed to not be influenced or controlled by her daughter's moods and to free herself from Tammy's efforts to set her father against her mother as an authority figure.

As with so many single parents who need to refute being controlled by guilt, Adele felt guilty and remorseful for Tammy's absent father. Tammy became an expert at manipulating the situation and, when she didn't get her way, she would threaten to run away and go live with her dad. In reality, her dad and his wife would have never allowed this.

Adele's Dysfunctional Thinking Process

These are the primary self-defeating thoughts that created Adele's resistance to taking charge of her daughter:

THOUGHT: "If I lose Tammy's approval, she won't like me."
COGNITIVE DISTORTIONS: All-or-none thinking. Magnification.
    Jumping to conclusions (fortune-telling).

THOUGHT: "I shouldn't be too firm or she'll live with her father."
COGNITIVE DISTORTIONS: Jumping to conclusions (fortune-telling).
   Should statement.

THOUGHT: "Tammy doesn't have a father model. It's obvious why she
   gets so angry when she doesn't get her way."
COGNITIVE DISTORTIONS: Jumping to conclusions (fortune-telling).
   Personalization and blame.

THOUGHT: "It's too late to set rules now. Things will never change."
COGNITIVE DISTORTIONS: All-or-none thinking. Jumping to
   conclusions (fortune-telling).

Using the ten cognitive distortions, Adele was able to dramatically
change her thinking process:

FROM: "If I lose Tammy's approval, she won't like me."
TO: "I need to step up as a parent. I need to put my feelings aside and do
   what's best as a parent. Initially, she may dislike me, but hopefully,
   she'll learn to respect me. Adolescents, underneath it all, need and
   want structure in their formative years."

FROM: "I shouldn't be too firm; she'll live with her father."
TO: "Tammy has been emotionally blackmailing me. If by chance her
   father takes her in, it won't be long until he sends her back. If she
   doesn't learn now that we all have consequences for our behaviors,
   she may never learn it. If that's the case, her future will be dismal. It
   won't be easy, but I need to step up now and be a parent."

FROM: "Tammy doesn't have a father model. It's obvious why she gets
   so angry when she doesn't get her way."
TO: "Even if she lived with her dad, his irresponsible, childish ways
   would be of harm to her. When she is ready, I will send her to
   counseling to help her work out her father abandonment issues. She
   is getting angry because, like children when they don't get their way,
   they have tantrums. Also, she doesn't have anger problems in school;

she has anger outbursts at home because she can get away with it. In the future, if she has an outburst at home, she will have a consequence. For her sake, I will take charge."

FROM: "It's too late to set rules now. Things will never change."
TO: "This won't be easy. I need to quietly seek emotional support from family members and friends to carry out rules with natural, logical consequences. I must remember dysfunctional families follow dysfunctional rules. By me changing and becoming more firm and establishing structure, she will change. I will start by taking small steps to implement change."

Adele was becoming more and more aware of how her thoughts were causing her resistance to being a responsible parent. This resistance led to her inability to properly discipline her child. She began to realize that when she felt anxious, sad, or angry, these feelings were the windows to her thoughts. Then she was able to make rebuttals before the thoughts spiraled her down to a deep state of depression (Law of Association).

She also was becoming quite skilled at using mindfulness in daily life. Each time she found herself thinking about Tammy and feeling anxious, angry, sad, or frustrated, she would utilize *Red Light/Green Light*.

- STOP: Breathe in deeply for four seconds and then out for eight seconds. Let myself become calm. Pay attention to myself.
- THINK: What's my old self-defeating pattern here?
- GO: Take purposeful action. What is my best choice of reactions in this situation?

Specifically, when Tammy would be disrespectful, Adele would give her a warning and say, "It's your choice. You can move away from me right now because if you continue with the disrespect, I am taking away your phone for the rest of the day and evening." Initially, as expected with any change, there were difficulties. But as time progressed, Adele gained confidence, and it became easier and easier for her to discipline Tammy. She charted her success (Law of Motivation) on a weekly basis and found it easier and easier to parent in a healthy way.

Adele began to project an image of a confident, in-control parent and, in turn, Tammy started adhering to Mom's rules and won Mom's respect (Law of Attraction). Adele persistently focused on what she wanted — to take charge of her daughter and be a responsible parent. Like so many teens, Tammy later admitted that deep down inside she wanted more structure in her life.

Two-Parent Families Have Difficulties, Too

Parents need to work together and back each other up in the difficult role of setting limits with natural, logical consequences.

— *Dan Hoffman, LCSW*

Two adults, working together at the tasks of parenting children, can have a definite advantage over a single parent, especially in dealing with the occasional outrageous behavior of a hormonal teenager. Parents need to work together and back each other up in the difficult role of setting limits with natural, logical consequences. As I discuss elsewhere, stepfamily parents need to take a different approach to raising children than families which include both biological parents. In two-parent families, the parents must work as a team to win the struggle for power that inevitably arises while raising children. It takes a lot of effort to consistently enforce the rules and consequences.

Many adolescent negative behaviors can be resolved, but some negative actions have life-long consequences. Adolescents' rebellious behavior is a normal part of their development process — or otherwise they would never leave the nest. This process often translates into a struggle for power with the parents. In their attempt to gain control over the rules that govern them, teens look for ways to circumvent the authority of their parents. When they find vulnerable areas in the boundaries set by their parents, they rush to seize power and overthrow parental control. How many times have you heard, "Why can't I go out? Randy's parents are letting him go." or "It's okay if I go out, Dad said so." or "Everybody can go to the party but me." Parents need to align and back each other up in setting firm limits and boundaries.

> Often, conflict expressed by the child is a reflection of the conflict between the parents.
>
> — *Dr. William Matta*

Too frequently, I see parents undermine each other when it comes to establishing mutually agreed upon rules with natural, logical consequences. Often, for unconscious reasons, a parent will side with the child to help the child win the power struggles. For example, a father whose mother was too controlling may unconsciously take the side of the child in mother-child clashes to defeat the mother. Conversely, a mother whose father was abusive may unconsciously rescue the child from the father whenever the father attempts to set limits for the child. Take a moment and reflect on how you and your spouse work together to set limits with your children. If you don't, or can't, work as a team, why not? Are there family-of-origin issues holding one of you back? How were you parented? How was your spouse parented?

Even when children are extremely young, ages two or three years, their behavior can reflect conflict between their parents. I have seen preschoolers be out of control because the parents' behavior was out of control. This occurs when parents are habitually fighting in front of the child and the house is in a constant state of upheaval.

Any discord between the husband and wife reverberates throughout the family. In such situations the parents tend to undermine each other, and the children tend to undermine the parents. When children can't or won't use words to express their feelings, they act them out. Just as adults can, children can act out anger, frustration, and fear in an attempt to get rid of unpleasant emotions.

Some parents have extreme difficulty in working together to establish boundaries. Why? Because we usually parent the way we were parented. If our parents were strict, we tend to be strict. If our parents were liberal, we tend to be liberal. And it's okay to disagree when discussing a difference of opinion about rules and boundaries so as long as your child is not aware of your discussion, but you need to compromise and project a united front to your child.

A Two-Parent Family: Maureen and Monroe

Maureen's alcoholic father was emotionally abusive to her, and no one came to her rescue. In an attempt to keep peace with her aggressive husband, Maureen's mother would turn her back on the abuse. When Monroe would make an effort to correct their teenage daughter Natalie, Maureen would often side with her daughter. Such actions would infuriate Monroe, which would only serve to reinforce Maureen's negative feeling toward men as role models. In the meantime, by dividing and conquering her parents, Natalie was able to get her way and circumvent the rules.

Maureen and Monroe entered counseling because they argued constantly and their daughter was out of control. They really had no idea about the nature of their conflict or why their daughter's behavior was out of control. They had no idea why or how the alignment between Maureen and Natalie was devastating the marriage and family life. After all, Maureen was only doing what she thought was best for her daughter — trying to rescue Natalie — while, in reality but on a hidden level, Maureen was attempting to rescue herself.

Maureen's central dysfunctional thoughts

Counseling brought Maureen to the realization that her family-of-origin issues were sabotaging her husband's attempts to enforce consequences for their daughter.

THOUGHT: "I can't expose Natalie to any abuse, even verbal abuse. I won't let it happen."
COGNITIVE DISTORTIONS: All-or-none thinking. Overgeneralization. Jumping to conclusions (fortune-telling). Magnification.

THOUGHT: "I'm the mother. I know what is best for my daughter, and anyway Monroe is too strict."

COGNITIVE DISTORTIONS: All-or-none thinking. Overgeneralization. Jumping to conclusions (mind-reading). Emotional reasoning. Personalization and blame.

THOUGHT: "Monroe and I will never agree upon rules with natural, logical consequences, I just know it."
COGNITIVE DISTORTIONS: All-or-none thinking. Jumping to conclusions (fortune-telling). Emotional reasoning. Personalization and blame.

Monroe's central dysfunctional thoughts

Monroe was also able to identify his negative thoughts:

THOUGHT: "Things will never change. She'll always side with her daughter."
COGNITIVE DISTORTIONS: All-or-none thinking. Overgeneralization. Jumping to conclusions (fortune-telling). Personalization and blame.

THOUGHT: "We'll never be able to discuss the use of natural, logical consequences for Natalie. I feel hopeless. There is no use trying."
COGNITIVE DISTORTIONS: All-or-none thinking. Jumping to conclusions (fortune-telling). Magnification. Emotional reasoning.

Maureen and Monroe eventually became proficient in using the ten cognitive distortions, reframing, and *Boulders, Rocks & Pebbles* to change their thoughts:

FROM: "I can't expose Natalie to any abuse, even verbal abuse. I won't let it happen."
TO: "Monroe and I need to sit down and discuss how we are going to present the rules with natural, logical consequences to Natalie in a calm, relaxed manner. As Dr. Matta said, she'll probably flip out when we discuss the matter, and that's when Monroe and I need to stay calm and in power. Even though I haven't been abusive to

Natalie in any fashion, somehow it hasn't stopped her from being abusive to me. Her abusive behavior must stop."

FROM: "I'm the mother, I know what's best for my daughter, and anyway Monroe is too strict."

TO: "Well, my way isn't working. Dr. Matta said it's imperative that I work with Monroe to establish mutually agreeable rules with natural, logical consequences. We can work it out."

FROM: "Monroe and I will never agree upon rules with natural, logical consequences. I just know it."

TO: "In the past, every time we tried to discuss establishing natural, logical consequences, it would turn into a major fight. We need to use the communication rules Dr. Matta taught us [as outlined in this book] and organize problem-solving conversations. We need to put aside our differences and work together for the sake of our daughter and our relationship."

FROM: "Things will never change; she'll always side with Natalie."

TO: "Maureen now understands that Natalie is out of control and that we have to do something. I think Maureen is coming around and will be willing to work with me for Natalie's sake. It's the only chance Natalie has to become a responsible part of this family."

FROM: "We'll never be able to discuss the use of natural, logical consequences for Natalie. I feel helpless, there is no use trying."

TO: "Maureen is not the same person she used to be; she's learning to be more open minded and less defensive. She now realizes that her inability to enforce consequences for Natalie had to do with her family-of-origin issues. Maureen now realizes the importance of enforcing consequences, if Natalie is to grow up to be a responsible person. We are now approaching the problem from a healthy perspective."

Prior to counseling, Maureen was never really aware how her pivotal thought to rescue her daughter served as a wedge between her and her husband, as well as why it was the major source of Natalie's oppositional behavior and the major reason for the couples' marital problems. Eventually, Maureen became aware of the relationship between her conditioned environmental triggers: disciplining her daughter in reaction to her anxiety and her anger toward her husband due to her dysfunctional thoughts that caused her resistance to proper parenting.

By utilizing the principles of mindfulness, Maureen was able to refute her negative thoughts before they caused her to despair. She even kept track of her behavioral improvements on a weekly basis which served to reinforce continued success (Law of Motivation). Eventually, Maureen and Monroe were able to take charge of their daughter.

SOLUTION SUMMARY

- Parents need to take charge of their children.
- Single parents have specific problems raising children alone, often arising from enmeshed early relationships.
- The agenda of the adolescent is to reform the parent.
- Dysfunctional families follow dysfunctional rules.
- Parents need to establish rules with natural, logical consequences.
- Two-parent families have issues, especially when the parents can't present a unified front.
- Discord between the husband and the wife reverberates throughout any kind of family.

12. Taking Charge of an Abusive Relationship

Daniel Hoffman, LCSW

Even if a woman was abused a very long time ago, it comes out in her life in a negative way.

— *Catherine Deneuve*

Law Enforcement and Counseling Perspectives on Abuse

My dual perspective on the topic of abuse comes from my two related careers: law enforcement and mental health counseling. For 25 years I served as a municipal police officer in Camden, New Jersey. Prior to my retirement from law enforcement, I attained the rank of Captain of Police. During my law enforcement career, I responded to many incidents of abuse wherein family members were either victims or perpetrators.

While in the Camden Police Department, I served on the Camden County Domestic Violence Working Group, a group composed of police administrators, judges, the County prosecutor, Family Court officials, the victim-witness coordinator, and various community leaders and officials. The group met on a regular basis to provide ongoing intervention and multi-agency cooperation in addressing the domestic violence crisis that was occurring in Camden County. Domestic violence is a problem across the nation as well as worldwide.[44]

In addition, for over 15 years I have provided counseling services to families where abuse is an issue, in community-based counseling agencies as well in my private practice, in locations in New Jersey and Florida. This chapter addresses the topic of abuse from a law enforcement perspective as well as a counseling perspective.

The Three Types of Abuse

> If the numbers we see in domestic violence were
> applied to terrorism or gang violence, the entire country
> would be up in arms, and it would be the lead story on
> the news every night.
>
> — *Mark Greene, congressman*

There are three basic categories of abuse in relationships: physical, emotional, and sexual. Let's examine these types.

Physical Abuse

Physical abuse happens when the physical actions of a person cause physical pain or injury to another person. Physical abuse also includes using the threat of physical force to intimidate the abused person. Examples of physical abuse include hitting, slapping, kicking, punching, pushing, throwing things at someone, choking, or holding a person against their will. Any time a person causes another to feel physical pain or injury, we have physical abuse. Living in fear on an ongoing basis is a hallmark of physical abuse.

To illustrate the severity of the problem of physical abuse in the United States, please review the following statistics regarding domestic violence:

- One out of four women is the victim of domestic violence in her lifetime.
- Almost three out of four people know someone who is a victim of domestic violence.

- On average in this country, four people are murdered in a domestic violence incident each day.
- It is estimated that 1.3 million women are victims of domestic violence each year.
- About 85% of domestic violence victims are women.

Emotional Abuse

A person is the recipient of emotional abuse when the abuser attempts to use guilt, humiliation, shame, fear, and other emotional manipulations to gain control over or intimidate the victim for any reason. Withholding affection or any form of human interaction for excessive periods of time, making false accusations, isolating the victim from family and friends, or otherwise denying the person sources of comfort and strength such as typical support groups or spiritual support are all forms of emotional abuse. When a person uses insults or verbal put-downs, sexist remarks, hurtful name-calling, racial slurs, constant yelling, or demeans a person's appearance, intelligence, or other personal traits, you have emotional abuse. In short, emotional abuse can be any action that affects someone's sense of emotional well-being.

Emotional abuse is particularly harmful because it's not always easy to detect objectively. Therefore, it may occur over long periods of time.

Sexual Abuse

Sexual abuse occurs when someone forcibly has sexual contact or any sexualized interaction with a person who is not consenting to such contact or interaction. Sexual abuse also occurs when someone has sexual contact or interaction with someone who is not able to fully consent due to mental or physical disability or age. Date rape and forced sexual activity between two cohabitating or married people is also sexual abuse, as long as one party is not consenting to the activity.

Some examples of sexual abuse:

- Forcible, unwanted sexual act
- Sadistic sexual acts without consent
- Being called sexually derogatory names

- Being criticized sexually
- Forced sex after physical abuse
- Taking unwanted sexual pictures or videos of the victim
- Forcing the victim into prostitution
- Forcing the victim to interact sexually with a third person

Signs of an Abusive Relationship

> One's dignity may be assaulted, vandalized, or cruelly
> mocked, but it can never be taken away unless it is
> surrendered.
>
> *Michael J. Fox*

In my law-enforcement career, I encountered many victims of abuse.
Most of the abuse I dealt with then was physical abuse. When I began my
mental health counseling career, I came to realize that emotional and
sexual abuse were also significant issues in our society. Oftentimes I
counseled someone who had been a victim of at least two of the three
forms of abuse. Any of these signs can indicate that you are possibly a
victim of some kind of abuse.

- Do you feel fearful or nervous around your partner?
- Are you very careful not to say or do anything that may make your
  partner angry?
- Are you afraid of disagreeing with your partner?
- Have you had sex with your partner because you were afraid to say
  "no"?
- Do you feel humiliated or criticized by your partner around other
  people?
- Do you feel you are not allowed to handle money?
- Are you constantly feeling your partner does not trust you?
- Do you get blamed for your partner's faults or behaviors?
- Does your partner make excuses for his or her behavior?
- Are you not allowed to communicate or interact with family or
  friends?

- Does your partner make you feel there is something wrong with you?
- Have you been fearful of being the victim of physical or sexual violence?
- Does your partner ever threaten suicide in order to manipulate you?
- Do you ever think of suicide during or after an abusive incident?
- Are family members, friends, or co-workers concerned about your safety and well-being?

Cycle of Physical Abuse

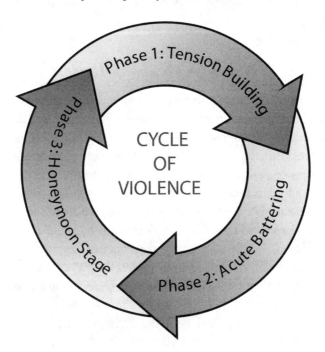

Phase One: Tension Building

Tension in the relationship begins to build as anger, blaming, and arguing escalate.

Phase Two: Acute Battering

In this phase, the abuser loses control and perpetrates physical violence or intimidation upon the victim.

Phase Three: Honeymoon Stage

During this phase, the abuser asks for forgiveness and often treats the victim nicely by doing things such as buying flowers, offering to spend quality time, or reminiscing about good times that the couple has had. The abuser also makes promises that the abuse won't happen again. Victim usually lets cognitive distortions fool them into believing that things will be different.

Sarah: A Victim of Abuse

Sarah provides a classic example of how abuse can have an ongoing effect. She contacted me to begin counseling and said that she was interested in couples counseling to work on marital issues. However, her husband was initially unwilling to attend sessions, so Sarah began attending sessions alone, upon my recommendation.

Sarah had been married to Tom for 13 years. This was her second marriage. During her first marriage, she endured trying to live with an alcoholic husband and after eight years that marriage ended in divorce. In the first session, I fully assess my new clients to get a picture of the important issues that may need to be addressed. When I got to the abuse section of my evaluation and asked if there were any abuse issues in her life, Sarah became tearful. After a while she was able to compose herself enough to report that she had been the victim of physical abuse by her first husband and that she believed that her current husband began emotionally abusing her after the birth of their first child. She said, "The abuse didn't happen all the time. It was only occasional with both husbands." She also spoke of her belief that her own behaviors tended to result in her being abused.

In light of my professional experience, I suspected that Sarah was a long-term victim of abuse. In the counseling field we find that such abuse is present in many relationships and follows a cyclical pattern.

Sarah and her husband would get along all right for a period of time. Then her husband would start to get moody and Sarah would begin to feel like she was walking on eggshells. Then her husband would become angry and abusive. And then, immediately after the abusive period, her husband would become very apologetic and the couple would get along for a while. This pattern occurred in both of Sarah's marriages and is a classic example of a cycle of abuse.

Sarah had first experienced abuse during her first marriage. Being in partnership with a person who is addicted to a substance or behavior often results in emotional abuse of the non-addicted partner. Sarah and her second husband often struggled financially due to the fact that he was not earning a regular income. Whenever these issues came up in conversation, he became angry and criticized Sarah's maintenance of their finances. Often he also was very critical of her appearance, her cooking, and how she cleaned the house. Typically, when Sarah would ask for help around the house, he would lose his temper, and sometimes he would throw things at her or punch the walls with his fists.

As Sarah and I worked together to sort out her issues, her pattern of dysfunctional thoughts came into her awareness.

Sarah's dysfunctional thoughts

THOUGHT: "I should have known better than to provoke him."
COGNITIVE DISTORTIONS: All or nothing thinking. *Should* statements. Personalization and blame.

THOUGHT: "If I do what he wants, he won't treat me so badly."
COGNITIVE DISTORTIONS: Minimization. Jumping to conclusions (fortune-telling).

THOUGHT: "I'm not fit to be in a relationship. This is my second failed marriage."
COGNITIVE DISTORTIONS: Personalization and blame. Overgeneralization. Emotional reasoning.

THOUGHT: "I should be able to take care of the household by myself."

COGNITIVE DISTORTIONS: All-or-none thinking. *Should* statements. Personalization and blame.

THOUGHT: "I don't deserve his help anyway."
COGNITIVE DISTORTIONS: Minimization. Jumping to conclusions (fortune-telling). Personalization and blame.

THOUGHT: "The abuse I get is not so bad that I can't handle it."
COGNITIVE DISTORTIONS: Minimization. Emotional reasoning.

During her counseling sessions, Sarah revealed that her self-defeating thoughts revolved around chronic low self-esteem. She came to realize that her thoughts were the source of her poor self-image. These thoughts prevented her from believing that she had an absolute right to not be abused. The Law of Resistance is applicable here: Sarah needed to identify the negative thoughts that were causing resistance to change by making her unwilling to make positive changes. We can see that cognitive restructuring of her dysfunctional thoughts will result in positive thoughts that will cause positive change.

FROM: "I should have known better than to provoke him."
TO: "I have the right to speak my mind. I expect him to communicate with me as a partner."

FROM: "If I do what he wants, he won't treat me so badly."
TO: "I deserve to be treated with fairness, to be treated decently."

FROM: "I'm not fit to be in a relationship. This is my second failed marriage."
TO: "I deserve a good relationship, no matter what my past experiences were."

FROM: "I should be able to take care of the household by myself."
TO: "My husband and I are equal partners and both of us need to pitch in to take care of things around the house."

FROM: "I don't deserve his help anyway."
TO: "I deserve to ask for help any time I feel I need it."

FROM: "The abuse I get is not so bad that I can't handle it."
TO: "No amount of abuse is acceptable. I have the right to never be abused."

I instructed Sarah on becoming aware of mental, emotional, and physical cues informing her that she was in the process of thinking dysfunctional thoughts. During counseling, she and I were able to identify these cues, which enhanced her awareness of her thought processes. Sarah would then follow my advice to breathe in deeply for four seconds and then breathe out for eight seconds, letting herself relax. Then the negative thoughts would start to decrease. She went on to learn to use the *Red Light/Green Light* technique.

Tom Begins Counseling and Makes Changes

After eight counseling sessions with Sarah alone, Tom decided to join the counseling process. In counseling, Tom was able to confront his habit of emotional abuse. He identified some cognitive distortions that were present at times and was able to develop the ability to refute those distortions. He began to regularly challenge his distorted thoughts and learned to use mindfulness techniques such as *Red Light/Green Light*. Sarah and Tom were able to salvage their marriage by developing good, ongoing communication skills as well as awareness of the dysfunctional thoughts that had led to repeated incidents of emotional abuse.

In the context of the four pivotal laws, Tom became increasingly aware that Sarah would no longer tolerate any abusive behavior and that she would leave him if he continued to be abusive. Deep down, he knew he was wrong in acting in such an abusive manner, like having a baseball bat nearby that could be used to manipulate her into submission. Out of desperation, he became more willing and able to recognize and stop self-defeating, aggressive thoughts before they thrust him into an angry, abusive mindset (Law of Association). He became able to reset his emotions.

For Sarah, success truly bred success as she became more confident and even more determined to set boundaries (Law of Motivation). As Sarah changed and rightfully stood up for herself, it became obvious to me that Tom came to the realization that she did not deserve to be the recipient of such childlike, threatening behavior (Law of Association). Both grew healthier.

The Three Stages of Recovery from Abuse

I must offer an important caveat here. Not all abusive relationships work out positively like Tom and Sarah's did. In a relationship in which one is being abused, whether physically, emotionally, or sexually, both must want to make a change in order for their relationship to thrive. If your partner is not willing to seek change, you must use all the resources from this book that you can to ensure that you stop being a victim and successfully recover from being abused. Although the following is written using female pronouns, the same information applies for men who are being abused.

> Another way to understand your healing journey is to think of growing from a place of "victimization" to "survival" and finally into "thriving."
> — *Susanne M. Dillman, Psy.D.*

The Victim Stage

The first stage is called the victim stage. This occurs when the victim realizes that she has suffered abuse. This stage is characterized by raw emotion and a flood of cognitive distortions that often express self-blame. The victim stage corresponds to *Red Light Mode*, in which the client is empowered to stop the dysfunctional thought process.

The Survival Stage

The second stage is the survival stage. During this stage the abused person will express less denial of the abuse and will develop a desire and commitment to explore how to stop the abuse. The survivor stage corresponds to *Yellow Light Mode.* Here the client will think of options and begin to take steps to leave the abusive relationship.

The Thriving Stage

The third and final stage is the thriving stage, when the abused person becomes aware of how having been in an abusive relationship has affected her thought processes. Her thought distortions become evident and the newly thriving person challenges these thoughts and replaces them with more functional thoughts. The thriving stage corresponds to *Green Light Mode.* In this stage the abused person has left a past abusive relationship behind and is less likely to be drawn into another abusive relationship.

> No woman has to be a victim of physical abuse. Women have to feel like they are not alone.
>
> — *Salma Hayek*

Survival Tools — Develop a Safety Plan

The topic of this chapter demands that I provide some concrete tools and suggestions that may be needed to implement change in cases of abuse. These tools and suggestions are not a guarantee of safety, but they could well be vital in improving your safety in an abusive situation. Any person who lives with the threat of violence or is a victim of ongoing abuse needs to develop a safety plan:

- Identify the safest location in your home or workplace. Avoid a room that does not offer an escape route. For example, many victims choose to retreat to a bathroom because they feel they can lock themselves inside to be safe. It is generally better to choose a room with more than one exit point. Avoid rooms with potential weapons, such as the kitchen, garage, or workshop.
- Make a list of safe places to go, such as a domestic violence shelter, police station, etc.
- Keep a means of communication nearby, such as a cell phone or other cordless phone.

- Go online and research safety plans for domestic violence — but don't use a computer that is shared with the abuser. Instead, use a computer in a safe place such as a library or friend's home. Once you are able to use a computer safely, you can develop your own personal safety plan.

Safety Plan Guidelines

> You are not alone and you won't have to fight this battle by yourself.
> — *Anonymous domestic violence survivor*

After you come to the decision that you have to get out of an abusive relationship, you need to leave in a safe and secure manner. At this critical time, you must be aware of possible retaliation. You have to develop a plan to help ensure that your exit will be accomplished safely. I have found the following suggestions to be useful in helping my clients maintain safety throughout the process of leaving the abusive relationship:

Personal safety while still living with the abuser

The first important step is to plan for how you will stay safe before you leave. Develop a plan that includes where to retreat while under attack and making sure potential weapons are secured.

Personal safety while getting ready to leave

Make certain that you have everything you need to accomplish your escape. You should have copies of important documents including pictures of your injuries and damage to property.

General guidelines for leaving an abusive relationship

Obtain a restraining order

A restraining order can also be called an order of protection. This is a legal injunction issued by the court that requires one specified person to refrain from contacting or otherwise interfering in any way — violently or non-violently — with another specified person. Violation of any part of the order requires that law enforcement agencies immediately take the perpetrator into custody. In many communities, a law enforcement agency can initiate a restraining order at any time of day. Please contact your local law enforcement agency to find out the details of their specific procedures.

Many abuse victims fear obtaining a restraining order because they've heard news reports that a perpetrator who was subject to an active restraining order still committed violence. In my years in law enforcement, I saw restraining orders used to prevent many potential incidents of violence. Many perpetrators are deterred from contact with the victim as a direct result of being served with a restraining order. But, unfortunately, a victim often will not obtain a restraining order because of fear-creating cognitive distortions.

Avoid communicating with the abuser

Do not communicate with the abuser in any way, except under secure circumstances such as supervised visits arranged by the court. Contact your local law enforcement agency to request that they stand by while you leave, so you can do so safely, without forced communication with the abuser.

Safety after leaving an abusive relationship

- Acquire job skills.
- Research the various kinds of public resources in your community that can help abuse victims.
- Keep a journal that documents the time, location, and circumstances of any assaults, threats, and violations of restraining orders.

Resources

- For immediate help, call 911.
- For support and guidance, call the National Domestic Violence Hotline, 1-800-799-SAFE. Their website address is http://www.thehotline.org/.

What Constitutes a Good Relationship

You don't develop courage by being happy in your
relationship every day. You develop it by surviving
difficult times and challenging adversity.

— Epicures

In contrast to abusive relationships, a healthy relationship has the following characteristics:

- The couple's relationship is based upon commitment. Both feel secure about the future of the relationship. There are neither threats of divorce nor fear of abandonment.
- Both people are equal partners and share power and control in the relationship.
- The partners respect and listen to one another. They tend to organize problem-solving conversations. Communication does not consist of survival of the fittest.
- The couple tends to compromise on parenting philosophies. Discipline issues are discussed and negotiated, and the end result consists of mutually agreed upon rules and natural, logical consequences.
- The spouses share their feelings. They trust each other and are concerned for each other's welfare and happiness. They tend to think in terms of marital best interest.
- The relationship is characterized by honesty and accountability. The couple is open, trusting, and trustworthy, admits mistakes and wrongdoings, and each accepts responsibility for his/her behavior.
- Each partner has a healthy communication style and the insight to tell the other partner what the first partner needs and is not getting. No one has to second-guess the partner's wants.
- They maintain an enthusiasm for each other's hobbies, friends, and work, and each one focuses on his/her own daily lives
- Neither spouse is isolated in the relationship. They each have friends and interests outside the relationship.

- The partners share responsibilities and chores. They mutually agree on a distribution of work that is fair to both people.
- The children feel safe and loved by both parents.

SOLUTION SUMMARY

- You can take charge of an abusive relationship, at least to the extent that you can leave one that doesn't change.
- There are three types of abuse: physical, emotional, and sexual.
- You can find signs that you are possibly in a physically, emotionally, or sexually abusive relationship.
- The cycle of violence has three stages: tension building, abuse, and honeymoon.
- Both sides in an abusive relationship have dysfunctional thoughts.
- There are three stages of recovery from abuse: victim stage, survival stage, and thriving stage.
- Plans need to be made to leave a relationship safely, including obtaining a restraining order.
- Characteristics of a good relationship are completely different from an abusive relationship.

A Parting Quote

Why live our life in chains, when we already have the
key.

— From the song, "We Already Gone," by The Eagles

You now have the solution, plus a blueprint to make permanent
changes and achieve a joyful, fulfilling, and rewarding life. Now is the
time to put the solution into practice.

Most people need to practice new ways of thinking in order to create
new habits. Popular wisdom suggests that it takes approximately 21 days
of consistent practice to establish new habits and behaviors.

I recommend that on a daily basis, you use the meditation procedure
outlined in Chapter 7 to visualize and rehearse this book's four laws and
principles. To further ensure your success, you may also find it helpful to
frequently review the chapter summaries and your journal.

Remember — you now have the tools to *emotionally reset* yourself.
Best of luck to you!

Appendices

A. Rules for Speakers and Listeners[45]

Important rules for speakers

Speaking clearly and thoughtfully is important to getting your points across.

- SPEAK ATTENTIVELY: Avoid distractions, TV, radio, etc. Maintain appropriate and direct eye contact and look for responses that indicate your partner is listening.
- STATE THE PROBLEM CLEARLY: Use "I feel…" statements.
- DON'T TALK TOO MUCH: Speak to the point and avoid drawn-out statements. This will give your spouse a change to clarify and reflect on what he or she hears from you. When you speak, don't use more than two or three sentences.
- ACCEPT SILENCE: Sometimes one of the best ways to make a point is to pause or use a period of silence after speaking. This allows you and your listener to digest what is being said.
- DON'T CROSS-EXAMINE: Avoid firing questions at your spouse when attempting to learn something during a conversation. Refute such thoughts as, "I know what he or she will say." You both agreed to start anew.

Important rules for listeners

Many couples do not actually hear what each other is saying. Good listening skills involve a clear understanding of what is being said. Other important rules for listeners to follow include:

- LISTEN ATTENTIVELY: Keep good eye contact with your spouse and acknowledge that you are hearing him or her.
- DON'T INTERRUPT: It's impossible to hear when you are making rebuttals or talking to yourself.
- CLARIFY WHAT YOU HEAR: Sum up or make clear with your spouse your understanding of what is being said at the end of a statement or phrase. This will aid you in getting the correct message. It is also important to admit when you don't understand something.
- REFLECT ON WHAT YOU HEAR: This is different from clarification. Reflection, as with a mirror, involves showing your spouse that you are aware of or understand what he or she feels.
- SUMMARIZE: Both spouses should always attempt to summarize their conversation so that they have a clear understanding of what has been discussed.

B. Stepparenting

Strategies for stepparents are different from the ones used by biological parents. Central to the blended family is the couple's lack of an equal relationship with the children. Only the biological parent fully understands the emotional tie between him or her and the child. On an unconscious level, the child often experiences terrible emotional pain and a feeling of loss from the other biological parent.

Here are some stepparenting strategies that I recommend:

- If you are a new stepparent, don't try to or expect to have a major hand in disciplining right away. If you do, your involvement will be greeted by anger and resentment.
- Recognize and respect the child's love for the other biological parent.
- Encourage — don't discourage — the child's relationship with the other biological parent.
- Include the other biological parent in all family events that revolve around celebrations of the child, such as religious rituals, graduations, awards ceremonies, school plays, birthdays, etc.
- Allow time — at least a few years — for a relationship with your stepchildren to solidify.
- Be aware of how your stepchildren's stages of development affect their relationships with you.
- In building the relationship, focus on small successes.
- Don't force the relationship or demand love from your stepchildren.
- Control feelings of resentment and jealousy when faced with the close biological bond between your spouse and his/her children.
- Don't expect to feel equally toward your children and your stepchildren.

- Build the relationship with each stepchild individually.
- Accept that stepfamily life is not smooth sailing.

C. Components of Intimacy

According to Dr. Luciano L'Abate,[46] the components of intimacy are

- SEEING THE GOOD: Each partner should be able to see the good in himself/herself and in their partner. Both should be able to say what is good about themselves and be able to express what they like about the other.
- CARING: A caring attitude toward oneself and the other is vital to a healthy relationship. Caring, which each spouse may define differently, can be shown in many ways.
- PROTECTIVENESS: The couple must take care of each other. When children are involved in the family, the couple must first take care of the couple's relationship. Any discord between the husband and wife will reverberate throughout the family. In order to have a happy and nurturing family, it is essential that the relational partners see to the needs of their own relationship. The couple must also protect themselves from outside forces, such as work, in-laws, employers, and hobbies. I see too many couples who don't take time for each other. No wonder these relationships are strained over a period of time.
- ENJOYMENT: Enjoyment refers to giving pleasure to oneself and to one another. Couples need to take time to enjoy activities that they *both* enjoy just for the sake of pleasure. Too often, one partner will play golf and the other partner will play tennis, and they rarely enjoy activities together. If a relationship is to grow, the couple has to do things as a couple and have fun, the way they did when they first got married.

- RESPONSIBILITY: In an intimate relationship, each person must take responsibility for problems that might occur in the relationship. Both partners are accountable for the relationship. Each partner is responsible for resolving problems in the marriage. Therefore it takes both parties to work out the difficulties. Too often, one partner blames the other for a problem. For example, a husband prefers to stay in the house and not to do things together outside the home. The wife needs to get out of the house once in awhile. I tell both spouses that they have not just the right but also the relational duty to tell their mate what they need from the relationship that they are not getting. Having "good reasons" to avoid the partner's needs — like exhaustion from working or parenting, lack of imagination, or an unwillingness to re-experience things — will not do the trick. Intimacy will only grow if you challenge yourself to move beyond your own comfort zone.

- SHARING HURT: Intense levels of anger are often characteristic of troubled relationships. Suppressing feelings such as hurt, anger, resentment, frustration, and guilt only tend to fracture the relationship. The couple needs to learn that in a good marriage it's okay to talk about anything. Learning to share hurt rather than burying it is critical in promoting the understanding and empathy that underlie intimacy. Talking to others helps to dissolve unwelcome feelings within us. Not talking to others about our difficult feelings leads to acting out our feelings in pantomime. The partner that feels angry needs to discuss these feelings with the other partner.

- FORGIVENESS: In a marriage we will, from time to time, hurt the other partner. It is impossible to be in a relationship for a period of time without occasionally hurting the partner. Also, at times, we fight with our partner to create emotional distance we feel we need. I tell couples that forgiveness is a natural outgrowth of love. All of us are human, and we need to learn how to forgive one another. I believe that if we don't let go of anger and forgive one another, the resentment will eventually eat us alive.

D. Checklist of Ten Cognitive Distortions[47]

- ALL-OR-NONE THINKING: You look at things in absolute, black-and-white categories.
- OVERGENERALIZATION: You view a negative event as a never-ending pattern of defeat.
- MENTAL FILTER: You dwell on the negatives and ignore the positives.
- DISCOUNTING THE POSITIVES: You insist that your accomplishments or positive qualities "don't count."
- JUMPING TO CONCLUSIONS: 1. Mind-reading: You assume that people are reacting negatively to you when there's no definite evidence for this. 2. Fortune-telling: You arbitrarily predict that things will turn out badly.
- MAGNIFICATION OR MINIMIZATION: You blow things way out of proportion or you shrink their importance inappropriately.
- EMOTIONAL REASONING: You reason from how you feel: "I *feel* like an idiot, so I really must be one." "I don't *feel* like doing this, so I'll put it off."
- *SHOULD* STATEMENTS: You criticize yourself or other people with *shoulds* or *shouldn'ts. Musts, oughts,* and *have tos* are similar offenders.
- LABELING: You identify with your shortcomings.
- PERSONALIZATION AND BLAME: You blame yourself for something you weren't entirely responsible for, or you blame other people and overlook ways that your own attitudes and behavior might contribute to a problem.

E. Body System Malfunctions Due to Anxiety

Mental

Thinking

- Difficulty concentrating
- Lose objectivity and perspective
- Racing mind and uncontrolled thoughts
- Difficulty reasoning
- Confusion
- Can't remember names or important ideas

Senses and Perceptions

- Self-consciousness
- In a daze, haze, fog, or cloud
- On guard

Concepts

- Repetition of fearful concepts
- Distortion of thoughts
- Frightening visual images (not hallucinations)
- Fear of losing control (going crazy, being unable to cope, injury, death, negative evaluation)

Emotions

- Alarmed
- Anxious

- Edgy
- Impatient
- Fearful
- Frightened
- Jumpy
- Jittery
- Nervous
- Uneasy
- Wound up
- Tense
- Scared
- Terrified

Behavior

- Immobility
- Hyperventilation
- Postural collapse
- Flight
- Halting or stuttering speech
- Impaired coordination
- Avoidance
- Restlessness
- Inhibition

Physical

Breathing

- Lump in throat
- Shortness of breath
- Bronchial spasms
- Difficulty getting air
- Rapid breathing
- Gasping
- Pressure on chest
- Shallow breathing

- Choking sensation

Heart

- Racing heart
- Decreased or increased blood pressure
- Faintness; fainting
- Palpitations
- Decreased pulse rate

Belly

- Heartburn
- Revulsion towards food
- Nausea
- Vomiting
- Abdominal discomfort
- Abdominal pain
- Loss of appetite

Nerves

- Tremors
- Generalized weakness
- Pacing
- Spasms
- Clumsiness
- Increased reflexes
- Wobbly legs
- Unsteadiness
- Rigidity
- Startling
- Insomnia
- Fidgeting
- Eyelid twitching

Urinary Tract

- Frequent urination
- Pressure to urinate

Skin

- Pale face
- Hot and cold spells
- Itching
- Flushed face
- Generalized sweating
- Sweaty palms

Notes

1. American Academy of Pediatrics. 2013. Teen Suicide Statistics. http://www.healthychildren.org/English/health-issues/conditions/emotional-problems/pages/Teen-Suicide-Statistics.aspx
2. Daniel G. 1998. *Change Your Brain, Change Your Life: The Revolutionary, Scientifically Proven Program for Mastering Your Moods, Conquering Your Anxieties and Obsessions, and Taming Your Temper.* New York: Three Rivers. 42.
3. Ibid., 43.
4. Ibid., 47.
5. Leaf, Caroline, Ph.D. "Affirmative Thinking." Affirmative Thinking. http://affirmativethinking.wordpress.com/science-of-affirmations-proof/. Leaf, Caroline, Ph.D. "Thought Life." Dr. Leaf http://www.drleaf.net/.
6. Chapman, Cathy, Ph.D., LCSW. "Affirmative Thinking." Affirmative Thinking. http://affirmativethinking.wordpress.com/science-of-affirmations-proof/. Chapman, Cathy, Ph.D., LCSW. "Strengthen Your Immune System." Ezinearticles.com. May 4, 2009. http://ezinearticles.com/?Strengthen-Your-Immune-System---Live-From-Your-Heart&id=2304151.
7. McLeod, Saul. "Stress and the Immune System." Simplypsychology.org. 2010. http://www.simplypsychology.org/stress-immune.html.
8. Lemonick, Michael D. "The Biology of Joy." *Your Body: The Science of You: The Factors That Shape Your Personality*, by Stephen Koepp and Neil Fine, 20-24. New York: Time Books, 2013.
9. Singer, Thea. "Perfect Dose of Stress." *Psychology Today Magazine*, March 2013, 78.
10. Fredrickson, Barbara. "Ready for Anything." *Scientific American Mind Magazine*, July/August 2013 by Stephen Southwick and Dennis S. Charney, 32-39.
11. Singer, Thea. "The Perfect Dose of Stress." *Psychology Today Magazine*, March 2013, 78.
12. Biswass-Diener, Robert, and Todd B. Kashdan. "What Happy People Do Differently." *Psychology Today Magazine*, July 2013, 57.

13. Ibid., 57.
14. Southwick, Stephen, and Dennis Charney. "Ready for Anything." *Scientific American Mind Magazine*, July 2013, 32-41.
15. Byrne, Rhonda. *The Secret*. New York: Atria Books, 2006. 31-32.
16. Biswass-Diener, Robert and Todd B. Kashdan. "What Happy People Do Differently." *Psychology Today Magazine*, July 2013, 57. A study by Todd Kashdan and Colorado State Psychologist Michael Stegers. 2003.
17. Kluger, Jeffrey. "The Pursuit of Happiness." *Time Magazine*, July 2013, 24. Report on a study by Dr. Yalem Rotenberg, MD, Ph.D., Tel Aviv University, 2013.
18. From Wayne Welton, *Psychology: Themes and Variations,* 6th edition (Belmont, CA; Wadsworth, 2004), p. 639, Figure 1.
19. Adapted from David D. Burns, MD, *Feeling Good: The New Mood Therapy* (New York: William Morrow & Company, 1980; Signet, 1981).
20. Dixit, Jay. "The Art of Now: Six Steps to Living in the Moment." *Psychology Today Magazine*, November 1, 2008, 64-69.
21. Crocker, Jennifer, and Jessica J. Carnevale. "Letting Go of Self Esteem." *Scientific American Mind Magazine*, September 2013, 27-32.
22. Fralich, Terry. *Cultivating Lasting Happiness: A 7-Step Guide to Mindfulness*. Eau Claire, WI: Pepsi, 2007.
23. Adapted from Terry Fralich, LCPC, *Cultivating Lasting Happiness. A 7-Step Guide to Mindfulness.* (Wisconsin: PESI-2007) & Lynn Johnson, Ph.D., *Happiness: How Positive Psychology Changes Our Lives.* (Cross Country Education, LLC, 2011).
24. Exercises are from Explanation of Navigational Priority Copyright © 1999-2005 by Lynn D. Johnson. Contact: Ljohnson@solution-consulting.com.
25. Stein, Joel. "Just Say Om." *Your Body: The Science of Keeping it Healthy.* New York: Time Books, 2013. 24. Book by Herbert Benson, MD *The Relaxation Response*. New York: Morrow, 1975.
26. Stein, Joel. "Just Say Om." *Your Body: The Science of Keeping it Healthy.* New York: Time Books, 2013. 24. Study by David Kabat-Zinn, Ph.D. University of Massachusetts Medical School.
27. Stein, Joel. "Just Say Om." *Your Body: The Science of Keeping it Healthy.* New York: Time Books, 2013. 24. Study by David Kabat-Zinn, Ph.D. University of Massachusetts Medical School.
28. Ibid., 26.
29. Ibid., 25.
30. Ibid., 26. Barbara Fredrickson Ph.D., University of North Carolina. Study of *Journal of Psychological Science*, 2013.
31. Ibid., 26.
32. Lemonick, Michael, D. "The Power of Mood." *Your Body: The Science of Keeping It Healthy.* New York: Time Books 2013. Study by Dr. Dennis Charney, Dean of Icahn School of Medicine, Mount Sinai of New York. 14.

33. Bourne, Edmund J. *The Anxiety & Phobia Workbook*, 6ᵗʰ ed. Oakland: New Harbinger (2015).
34. Lemonick, Michael, D. "The Power of Mood." *Your Body: The Science of Keeping It Healthy*. New York: Time Books, 2013. 14. Study by Dr. Dwight Evens, Chairman of Psychology, University of Pennsylvania, & Dr. Dennis Charney, Dean of Icahn School of Medicine, Mount Sinai of New York.
35. Ibid., 12. Study by Dr. Dennis Charney, Dean of Icahn School of Medicine, Mount Sinai of New York.
36. Ibid., 12.
37. Ibid., 13.
38. "The Power of Mood." *Your Body: The Science of Keeping It Healthy*. New York: Time Books, 2013. Study by Dr. Bruce Cohen, President of McLean Hospital, Belmont Mass.
39. The Power of Mood." *Your Body: The Science of Keeping It Healthy*. New York: Time Books, 2013. *British Journal of Health* 2013. Paper by Tamlin Consen, University of Utago, New Zealand. "Mind-Boosting Remedies"
40. From: Kent Crockett, *Slaying Your Giants*. For more information see kentcrockett.blogspot.com/2013/06/the-thought-analyzer-test.html.
41. Sherman, Robert, and Norman Fredman. *Handbook of Structured Techniques in Marriage and Family Therapy*. New York: Brunner/Mazel, 1986. 16-19.
42. Steinberg, R. J. "Triangular Theory of Love." In *Psychological Review*, *93*, 119-35.
43. Hansen, James, and Luciano L'Abat. *Approaches to Family Therapy*. New York: McMillan Publishing, 1982. 167.
44. Statistics for this chapter from domesticviolenceandabuse.weebly.com/statistics.html and www.safehorizon.org/page/domestic-violence-statistics-facts-52.html
45. From: *Innovations in Clinical Practice: A Source Book*. Professional Resource Exchange, Sarasota, FL, and Beck, A. T. (1988). *Love is Never Enough*. Harper & Row, New York.
46. Adapted from: L'Abate, L. (1977). Enrichment Structured Interventions with Couples, Families and Groups. Washington, D.C. University Press of America.
47. Adapted from David D. Burns, MD, *Feeling Good: The New Mood Therapy* (New York: William Morrow & Company, 1980; Signet, 1981).

About the Authors

Dr. William Matta is a licensed psychotherapist in private practice for over 20 years. He is also an adjunct college psychology professor for over 25 years. His critically acclaimed book, *Relationship Sabotage: Unconscious Factors That Destroy Couples, Marriages, and Family,* is part of world-renowned media/radio/TV psychologist Dr. Judy Kuriansky's *Sex, Love, and Psychology* book series; has been embraced by numerous universities including Harvard, Princeton, and Cornell; and is recommended by Phoenix University and in Natalie Howard's selection of "good reads."

Dr. Matta has served on the New Jersey State Board of Marriage and Family Therapists for 23 years. He is included in *Psychology Today Magazine*'s list of America's best therapists. He is a certified hypnotist and has conducted many hypnotherapy seminars sponsored by hospitals, colleges, businesses, and schools.

Dr. Matta is a preferred child/adolescent provider for the Children's Hospital of Philadelphia (CHOP). He successfully treats adults for depression and anxiety by utilizing the methods described in this book, *The Solution: A Blueprint for Change and Happiness.* Dr. William Matta has been married for 41 years, has two children and three grandchildren, and resides in Southampton, New Jersey.

Daniel Hoffman, LCSW, retired as a captain from the Camden City, NJ, Police Department. During his 25-year career in urban law enforcement, he saw firsthand the effects of addictions and family dysfunction. After retiring from the police department, he continued his education and graduated from Rutgers University with a master's degree in social work (MSW). He is a licensed clinical social worker and has a private consulting practice in Florida. He has worked with many individuals and families who have suffered the effects of family dysfunction and addiction. He also provides training and consultation services to a variety of public and private organizations.